The Language
of the Study
# of Religion

The Language
of the Study
of Religion

A Handbook

George Weckman

To order additional copies of this book, contact:
Xlibris Corporation
1-888-7-XLIBRIS
www.Xlibris.com
Orders@Xlibris.com

Contents

1 WHAT, WHY, AND HOW 7
2 "RELIGION" 18
3 THE OLD RELIGIONS 31
4 THE NEW RELIGIONS 44
5 NON-RELIGION 58
6 THE STUDY OF RELIGIONS 70
7 RELIGIOUS EXPERIENCE 82
8 RELIGIOUS LANGUAGE 92
9 THEOLOGY AND
   RELIGIOUS LITERATURE 107
10 GOD LANGUAGE 119
11 HUMAN BEINGS 133
12 MORAL ACTIVITY 144
13 RITUAL ACTIVITY 154
14 SOCIAL PATTERNS 166

1 | WHAT, WHY, AND HOW

This is a book about language. It is a study of words and their use by speakers of the English language. It is about those words which are used to describe an important arena of human activity, i.e. religion, but it is only indirectly concerned with that activity. Religious thought and behavior are of primary interest to most readers of this book; that is why they use the words with which this book is concerned. However, let there be no confusion on this point: No matter what the ultimate aims of writer or readers, the following pages contain words about words—that is all, and that is enough.

Another way of putting it: This book is about "religion," not religion. The use of quotation marks in instances like this signals that a word is not being used in its common referential sense but is itself the focus of discussion. Such quotation marks will be a common sight on the following pages as we labor to dissociate the referent from the reference. In everyday speech, we rarely reflect on it; automatically, we think about the world and try to deal with it as it appears to us by using the familiar words of our cultural environment. The relatively few occasions when confusion arises at the level of common daily affairs are quickly resolved. It takes deliberate effort and deepened sensitivity to concentrate on the medium of the message instead of the message. The use of quotation marks should help to alert us to the shift in focus.

Perhaps this shift can be understood by an even more explicit use of the analogy to sight. The word "focus" already indicates that analogy of knowledge and sight, and it is very ancient and common in our language ("I see," we say, when we mean, "I understand"). We normally concentrate on finding the keyhole or avoiding the pothole as we use our eyes, but should our eyes or eyeglasses fail to function properly we become aware of their role in seeing and of the need to repair or adjust them. Likewise, people have been tripping around the realm of religiosity for a long time and there is great need for examining the lenses of our perceptions in that area. It would be so much easier if we could point to the things we are naming. But what do you point to, touch, or even smell when you want to indicate the references of most religious words? Angels and heavens are difficult enough, not to mention grace or karma. If you have not found it to be true yet, it will be obvious soon that the words used to understand religion and religions are among the most elusive kinds of words. They are abstract, ambiguous, and almost inevitably out of focus.

This is a book about the English language. There are similar problems in other languages but the details are different. Much said here about English might be applicable more directly to other Western languages but probably much less applicable to more distant or ancient languages where other words and other kinds of confusions occur. There is a special vexation here: The differences between languages prevents us from assuming that anything said here about English applies to other languages, yet in any attempt to understand humanity as a whole, data from other languages is necessary. Therefore, our concern with English words must lead us to consider how English words are used to translate words in other languages and also to note the introduction of foreign language words into English vocabulary.

Speakers of English, like speakers of any other language, want to understand everything in the world. It is most unlikely, however, that any language, let alone any one speaker, is adequate to the task of universal understanding. We must accept the fact of our limitation without ceasing to combat it whenever possible. That means in this context that we must recognize the limitations inherent in English as a basic fact, but also attempt to expand, change, and deepen the language at every point where that limitation is discovered. Even those rare individuals who know two or more languages from different language families and different parts of the world are not thereby relieved of the limitations of language; to the contrary, they become more aware of them.

Because this is a book about English it will have to examine, in addition to the problems of language limitation in general, the very specific characteristics of the English language, both good and bad. In the midst of what might seem to be some negative comments about English—an examination that must be more concerned with its difficulties than with its successes—I hope that it will be apparent that English is a wonderful language with many fine qualities. If all goes well, the pursuit of a study like this one is at the last more encouraging than discouraging. I love this language. Love can grow in the discovery of faults, or better, one can gain a love deeper than blind admiration by cherishing blemishes and weaknesses along with beauties. In any event, many people in this world understand things by structuring them in English words and sentences. So, whatever its faults, our goal is to work with this language as well as possible.

This is a book, furthermore, about academic English. I do not mean to say that these words are restricted to students and teachers, but that we need to be aware of them as they are also used in the deliberate and reflective investigation and explanation of religious matters. Although the words themselves may be found in many contexts, we are concerned here with their use in the study of religion. We shall reflect more as we proceed, on the ways in which people use these words to interpret just what religion is and religions are.

It is important to recognize that this book is not basically about religious language but about the language used to describe religion. The words used by people when they speak religiously are themselves interesting, and will concern us in part. However, the main problem of this book is the terminology used by students, at all levels of scholarship, to explain their own or someone else's religion. Thus it is primarily a matter of academic rather than believers' language.

The language used in the study of religion is problematic for a number of reasons, some of which are common to other areas of investigation and some of which are peculiar to the field of religion studies. In many disciplines common words are used in special ways within the conversations and writings of scholars. This specialists' jargon may be a matter of some dispute within the field in addition to being confusable with ordinary usage. It is also the case in most academic disciplines that the very process of naming and categorizing is a matter of interpretation, selection, and theory. Obviously, then, key words will be used in different ways by proponents of different theories or methodologies within the same field.

All this is true of the study of religion, plus some other things that are less obvious (though not absent) elsewhere. Especially detrimental, although understandable, is the process of using the terminology of a familiar religion to name the aspects of a foreign or ancient example. Much of what follows will consist of warnings about taking superficial cross-cultural similarities seriously without a great deal of testing and comparing. It is, nevertheless, inevitable that one will approach the unknown on the basis of the known. This has produced the situation in which a set of words derived from one religion (mainly Christianity, in English) provides the terminology for describing all other religions. That is bound to create the impression in the minds of some sincere students that they have come to know some other religion when actually what has happened is that the familiar words have camouflaged the new religion and have made true understanding all the more difficult.

As if all this were not problem enough, we also have to realize that religions themselves use language in special ways and this also affects academic usage. One of the reasons why the language of religious people is confusing is that they (like most of us) resist change. People do not like to give up the old ways and patterns even when they become quite dysfunctional. It is common, therefore, for the advocates of change in a religion to veil that change under the guise of a (new) interpretation of an old word. The interpretation turns out to be an innovation but it is argued as if it were a latent, hidden, but ever-present meaning in the word from the beginning. Scholars sometimes make themselves unpopular among believers in the religion in question when such shifts in meaning are demonstrated, but neither the process nor its discovery are necessarily unethical. Instead, it is academically most ethical to uncover the verbal maneuvers of human minds and languages in the quest for greater understanding of humanity.

Religions with sacred texts are especially vulnerable to this kind of maneuver. By insisting that the words and sentences in the ancient sacred texts really do not mean exactly what everybody may have thought that they meant, one can introduce something new and say that it is old at the same time. Of course this causes confusion regarding the meaning of the words within the religious tradition and certainly extends that confusion when such words are applied to other religions. Think of how many meanings the word "god" has for an example of this phenomenon of reinterpretation.

However, the worst problem in the study of religion and its terminology, more dangerous than anything mentioned so far, is emotional involvement. Some readers of this book, I suspect, are already disturbed by the tone of some of the preceding paragraphs. If they have held dear certain opinions about religion in general or their particular religious tradition, it may have seemed callous if not impious to speak about religious matters in cool, objective, and even bemused tones. I have tried to introduce some notes of humor into this discussion in hopes of vitiating the deadly seriousness with which religion is often addressed, and yet I also understand that many people might find such banter offensive. Others, of course, might find some passages too reverential. Talk about religion is a no-win situation; emotions run high on all sides. My deliberate aim in choosing words for these sentences is to avoid as much as possible all emotions except the desire for clarity and fairness. If this book contains somewhat impolite or jovial talk, it will be directed at myself, my tradition, and my culture, under the assumption that the only proper object of satire is oneself. We English-speaking intellectuals (into which group I gratuitously place myself and all my readers) are regularly appalled and amused by the silliness and the prejudice that has marred so much of religions and the study of religion. Nevertheless, we must remain engaged respectfully in the pursuit of better understanding, not denying the ultimate seriousness of the task.

The task is serious! The world is full of religious tension and even outright war. Much of this strife is due to real differences of belief, firmly held on each side. In this case participants and bystanders need to know what is going on lest they become involved in a way that they do not intend. Much strife, however, may be due to semantic confusion, and that is sad because it is avoidable. At one level this book is intended to aid the person who reads about religion to understand such writing more easily. At a deeper level, it is my fond hope that clarity about religions and an objective attitude in the study of religion will be advanced by the content and style of this book. I hope that respect and tolerance might thereby become more common in matters religious. In that case religious strife will not only be better understood but perhaps also diminished.

An objective attitude is probably indivisible from an intellectual and emotional posture which sees all religions as reasonable in their various ways. It is also usually connected to the proposition that it is impossible to know or to prove religion is ultimately true. This position is not necessarily anti-religious, but it is not characteristic of all religious people, to be sure. There are three kinds of personality involved here. Some believers and some critics of religion are very sure that they have the absolute truth, and summarily reject all other positions. The alternatives to their truths they consider to be dumb or demonic. A second group consists of the many believers and non-believers who do not think they can ever be sure that they have the absolute truth. Those in the second group will find it easier to develop the attitude of respect and tolerance toward all peoples and their beliefs. They suspend judgement indefinitely. Thirdly there are those who are sure that theirs is the only truth but study other religions anyway. They take the approach recommended here as a way of understanding how people and religions have made the mistakes they have made. That is, they may understand the academic study of religion as an attempt to see others less in terms of stupidity and perversity and more in terms of confusion and shortsightedness.

Whatever one's stance, despite the great difficulties involved, this project is dedicated to the ideal of fair and equal treatment of all peoples and their religions. This book might contribute to movement towards that ideal of fairness by improving our use of words and our understanding of the words of others. This is a high goal, never completely realizable. If we can move a little bit closer to it, if we can make our communication on the subject of religion even a little bit clearer and fairer, it is worth the effort.

I subscribe to the position that knowledge is a human construct, which may or may not have anything to do with reality, "what is out there," whatever the field of investigation. At the same time, however, this position can admit that there are various ways of testing such constructs to see whether they seem to fit or work. In some fields of study these tests are numerous and obvious such that we can begin to have great confidence in our thoughts about the world. Physics, Chemistry, and the like seem to be more verifiable than many other areas of human inquiry. At the other extreme lies the field of religion. Here I am not thinking of the unverifiability of religious beliefs, but of the unverifiability of theories and interpretations concerning the phenomenon of believing and acting religiously. It is one thing to say that gods, heavens, souls, and so forth are not demonstrable, and that has already been affirmed as a basic premise of this book. It is yet something else to affirm that the theories and scholarly concepts used to study religion are also barely demonstrable; but that too is a basic premise of this book. Even our theories about myths are almost mythical constructs, for example, but we must try to handle them carefully, like scientific hypotheses, until we can become somewhat confident that they are useful and that they fit the world to some degree.

We do not want to get too discouraged about this, but we cannot proceed realistically without admitting it: People's theories about religion in general and about particular religious phenomena are very difficult to test or verify. Some things can be asserted on the basis of central texts, very common practices, or historical consensus, but most items are simply too complex or ambiguous. It will be very apparent as we move on to specific words; beyond the ambiguity of words is the ambiguity of the subject matter. The total problem is not only one of semantic difficulty, because the conceptions or data to which our words supposedly refer are as much, if not more, in question than the word choice is. It is sufficient for the purposes of this study just to be clear about what people say religion is or religions are, leaving what actually exists to a different kind of investigation.

We can make a virtue out of this difficulty. The theories people hold about the nature of religion usually tell us more about the theorists than the supposed object of their theorizing. It is almost as vital and interesting to study theories about religion as it is to study the religions themselves. This study of others' theories illuminates our own efforts. Recognizing the extent to which the theories of past generations now seem so inadequate and biased should make us more modest. It should at the same time inspire us to greater effort and broader awareness in our struggles toward better understanding.

After these reflections on the theoretical nature of religion studies in general, let us return to the primary issue here, our problems with words. I discover in my students, my reading, and in myself a resistance to the fact that words can have more than one meaning. Every dictionary displays this fact in the lists of meanings it provides, especially for common words. Despite this, we find ourselves again and again searching for the correct or true meaning of a word as if the very existence of the word is guarantee of a single conception in comparison to which the other usages of that word are mistaken. Words that approach the ideal of single reference will figure very little in this book. Instead, we shall concentrate on words which have a variety of meanings, all more or less common.

For the most part, it will not be possible to say that one of the common definitions of a word is clearly better than another, just that it is not the same as the others. One definition or usage may be more appropriate or helpful in one context, and another in another. If we consciously avoid the tendency to settle on one definition to the exclusion of all others it is no longer necessary to show how weak or wrong the others are. On occasion it may be helpful to note the background or possible applications of a certain definition or approach, and in most instances a combination of definitions will be needed in order to understand or use the term effectively. As you read this book do not expect the complexity of language about religion to be simplified, only clarified.

Given the ambiguity of words, especially in the field of religion studies, is there any limit to the list of possibilities for meaning or significance? Yes and no! In all the word studies in this book, the list of meanings is partial and open-ended. People have meant and will mean much more by these words than can be summarized here. Only the most common and obvious senses are reviewed in this short book. There are, by consensus, reasonable limits to what words should be forced to do, Lewis Carrol's Humpty Dumpty notwithstanding. He formulated what people often practice, "When I use a word . . . . it means just what I choose it to mean—neither more nor less" (*Through the Looking Glass*). For our purposes here, however, a usage or meaning for a word must attain a certain prominence and popularity before it is worth taking into consideration. The meanings I review in these pages are the ones that seem most common and interesting to me, which means that I will miss some dimensions of some words that others find more attractive, more common, or both. I will do my best, and readers can supplement my comments with additions from their communities of speakers.

If words are so volatile and fluid, and if their use does not reflect the world but rather the user's construction of a model, how can we find any firmer ground on which to build our analysis? It would seem that ultimately Humpty Dumpty is right: Any word can mean anything, and it is a wonder that we think we communicate at all. My response to that pessimism might seem strange, but more words seem to help. If key terms in isolation are very ambiguous, they become less and less so as we place them in context and talk about them. There is a kind of meta-language function in the use of ordinary language to explain other language, other words. The problems do not vanish but they become less troublesome as we talk more about them. Therefore, these words about words should bring us closer to agreement about how words are used by people, singly and together, in their conceptualizations of the world of religion, even though those conceptualizations may or may not be good models of the actual religiosity of humanity.

The word-studies that follow will take a number of forms. In some instances, a history of the word, its etymology, may be useful and informative. This is not always the case because words have a peculiar kind of history which is not as logical as we might like it to be. Some definers of words are distracted by the etymology, struggling to make a connection between the original and current uses of a word when the connection is tenuous or unilluminating. In this book, for each prominent term, the various meanings will be identified or defined by using other, preferably non-technical, words. Each usage, meaning, or context of a word will be identified with a community of speakers insofar as that is possible. This might involve noting the medium or social framework within which such a usage prevails. It will be helpful also to take note of any implicit judgments or ulterior motives which might be involved in each usage. Finally, some examples are given that might clarify the various usages, illustrating what might be included or excluded from a category, the kinds of things apparently referred to by the term. These examples will be derived from the stock of experience of the average, somewhat educated American, insofar as I can anticipate what that experience includes.

Such word-studies may be of help to someone quite conversant in the field of religion studies, perhaps as a review or summary. The rank beginner with no background at all may find it all confusing at first and may not appreciate the distinctions or find them valuable. It is my conviction, however, that many people in the early stages of serious reflection on the religious behavior of human beings will find their way to knowledge eased and abetted by these exercises in definition.

Most of what is said here can be found in various dictionaries of religion, philosophy, or the English language. Often I find such books and their entries to be less analytical (often more historical or bibliographical) than is most helpful. Furthermore, dictionaries are not read as much (or heeded as much) as they should be. Only a few word-lovers spend as much time with the dry, telegraphic lists of meanings in dictionaries as words deserve. I hope that the discussions which follow inspire their readers to more frequent reference to dictionaries, encyclopedias, and the like. If I am successful, no one who follows these investigations will be able to use any of the words studied in a casual way any more. I hope also that the whole realm of words, the fabric of thought and knowledge, will become a more self-conscious element in the reader's intellectual life.

2 | "RELIGION"

The first big problem word in the study of religion is "religion." It is the vaguest, most comprehensive term; it is the one most often abused to serve some special interest. The extent and character of the subject matter of the religious studies field is determined by one's definition. Obviously it is necessary to come to some kinds of conclusions about the meanings of the word, even if those conclusions are very tentative, before any other intelligible statement in this field can be made.

First, we should be aware of some of the pitfalls. As with other words, many people have an ulterior purpose in defining religion a certain way. There are those who want to win arguments about how good or bad one religion, or religion in general, is. In this situation it is very clever to define the operative term in such a way that all religion or a particular religion turns out to be as good or bad as you want it to be. Examples include those who define the entire category of religion as a response to the fear of death or as the search for forgiveness, each of which is partial and prejudiced.

There are also a large number of people who do not feel comfortable with the lack of precision in discussions of religion. Instead of trying to bring clarity to the variety of meanings this word can have, as this book is dedicated to doing, they pounce on one meaning and declare all the others weak, wrong, or misguided. Although often a well-intentioned effort to cut through the confusion, ultimately it only covers up the problem. Beware especially of the system builders! They construct a pattern for sorting out the variety of human experience and try to sell it to the rest of us. Some of these systems are quite elaborate and useful, but they oversimplify. They put religion into some particular stage of human development or type of mentality, reorienting all the evidence and experience of religion so that it corroborates that role in their system. Even if you like such a system you will have to agree also that not everyone else does. When others say "religion" they may not mean what the systematizer thinks they should, and you will not understand them if you think they do.

Enough of these preliminaries! What sorts of things does the word "religion" mean in English? This word illustrates the uselessness of some etymologies. It seems to be derived from Latin *religare*, to bind, tie, fasten, but we cannot demonstrate that. Latin also has the word *religio* which means respect, awe, worship of sacred things. A lot of fanciful speculation has produced possible connections between these words, but it is also possible that they are unrelated. The stages of development which produced the Latin *religio* are inaccessible to us. If there was a connection between *religio* and *religare*, it may have been accidental and is therefore of no use in examining the concepts of religion.

The meanings of religion, however, do indicate one family of thoughts, by their usage to indicate a type of emotion, or acts associated with a certain emotion like awe. Certainly many English speakers and theorists find it convincing to root all the rest of what might be called religion in a specific kind of experience or set of experiences. We could say that these are the psychological definitions of the word. They tend to think of religion as individual and personal (although a mass psychology might be involved). They tend to subordinate the intellectual, ritual, and social phenomena of religions to the psychic or emotional, and to think of these as derivative from impressive, special experiences of the individual. These may be personal and direct or part of one's participation in a group and dependent on other people's inspiration and example. In either event for this definition, the origin and source of all that can be called religion comes from the realm of emotions, feelings, or unusual states of mind.

In this survey of definitions of religion I shall use as a handy pattern of nomenclature the fields of study and the areas of human existence upon which they focus, for example psychology. This will be used as a device for distinguishing the various definitions. Obviously not all psychologists or every psychological theory would adopt a definition of the kind that I am presenting, but some have. Furthermore, the adjective "psychological," and other similar word formations, can be understood to refer either to the discipline and its students, or to the object of study, in this case those aspects of human life which are mental and emotional. The psychological definition with which we have begun will be followed by discussions of sociological, anthropological, philosophical, and theological definitions. Even then, we will not have exhausted the possibilities, but will have a better feel for their range and variety of the definitions of religion.

Psychological definitions have been attractive in recent times because they seem to remove the essence of religion from arenas in which unsettling conflicts arise. The belief systems, social patterns, and ritual behavior of many prominent religious traditions do not seem to fit in well with the modern world, and yet these traditions continue to be influential and are widely practiced. This leads many to affirm a kind of fall-back position, that the essence or true nature of religion is not to be found in many of the kinds of human activity usually associated with the word. Instead one should look in that private area of life which seems to be less challenged or affected by modernity. I am suggesting that this is the reasoning behind the popularity of the psychological definitions.

The psychological definition comes in both positive and negative forms, as we will come to expect of many of these words. Those who are sympathetic to traditionally religious things, ideas, or people espouse a psychological definition which finds many of the operative emotions to be good. Certainly they may think that some gods do not deserve the awe and respect they sometimes get, but awe, respect, the desire to worship—all these can be evaluated positively. It will also be a matter of subsidiary judgment to decide what and how much emotion is better or worse—visions and ecstasies or the lack thereof can be variously recommended, all within the common framework wherein religion is a matter of the heart, as they say, and is good.

There are those who define religion in psychological terms, however, who are far less complimentary of religions. This approach interprets religious emotions in light of the plausibility of their aspirations or the effects they have on life. If religious emotion is understood as confidence in will-o'-the-wisps or as childish desires, then it does not seem very admirable or is at least a sign of immaturity. Insofar as religions may offer forgiveness, transcendence of the normally human, or life after death, this kind of view sees such possibilities as reactions of fear, wish-projection, self-delusion, and similar understandable but foolish creations of human imagination. The mature, healthy individual should not have to adopt the crutches of religious consolation and is better off without them, within this perspective.

The tables can be turned on this view of religion as childish and psychically unhealthy. There are a few theorists in the field of psychology and psychoanalysis for whom religions or religious phenomena can be elements in attaining maturity rather than escapes from it. This opinion has been so much identified with one man that it seems appropriate to identify him: C. G. Jung. In his view, religious symbols, activities, myths, etc. often (but not always, of course) aid in the process of maturation. Religions are seen to be reservoirs of resources for the individual's use in coming to terms with self, parents, the rest of humanity, and the human condition.

Let us turn next to sociological approaches to religion. The role of religions in educating the young and aiding their adjust-

ment to the demands of life is prominent in sociological definitions and theories. For the sociological definition, society and its
needs are seen to be the hidden force and plan behind religious
phenomena. Every society needs the effects which stable religions produce, even if at times religious impulses become
disruptive or even anti-social in their immediate effects. Religions are therefore understood as systems which are socially
useful because they interiorize the values and demands which
people must respect in order for the society to function. Religion
is defined as a dynamic of human social character, somewhat
like the herding instincts of animals and similarly effective because it helps preserve the species.

A sociological definition of religion selects a different arena
of human activity upon which to base its definition than does the
psychological or any of the other possibilities yet to be summarized. For this view it is the ethical norms, patterns of authority,
and group dynamics which are the basic, essential, determinative elements in anything generally called a religion. Special
personal experiences or individual psychic growth are accord-
ingly understood to be derivative or secondary to the social
function. The psychological approach as isolated in the discussion above reverses these elements, but there are also many
mixtures of the two.

Neither psychological nor sociological approaches satisfy
most religious believers or many students of religion. They are
accused of being reductionistic (more on this word in chapter
six), in that they tend to ignore what religious people actually say
and do, proposing a hidden purpose or meaning which the scholar
must uncover. In order to be more appreciative of the believer's
point of view, other definitions of religion have been developed
which try to be attentive to the aims and statements of religious
people. Following the pattern of naming the definitions of religion by areas of study, we can associate the first of these approaches
with the field of anthropology. The student of the foreign cultures
which are very different from the modern West is often struck by
other peoples' separation of the world into ordinary and special,

profane and sacred, natural and supernatural. A lot of different doctrines or theories are associated with that dichotomy but the dichotomization pattern remains structurally similar throughout many cultures. The essential thing about religions from this perspective is the positing of, and care for, some special set of things, ideas, places, etc. Whether or not we understand or sympathize with the basis of selection or the things selected, the point is that people segregate what they consider to be the powerful or significant elements of their lives from the ordinary and in so doing manifest their religion.

At first this dichotomization of the world into sacred and profane might sound like a superficial characteristic upon which to base a definition of religion but it turns out to be so widespread and crucial an element that it has served fairly well as a common denominator of all the variety in the world's religions. The words *mana* and *taboo* have become common in English from the fascination of Westerners with strange native practices. Having seen this attitude in unfamiliar contexts and with unusual contents, the application to Western culture and religion was expectable and proved illuminating. Perhaps it should not have been surprising that almost every culture, upon close inspection, revealed its *mana* and *taboo*, that is, its ritual and intellectual bifurcation of the world.

The important thing in such an approach to the meaning of religion is its focus on structure, not content. The object of deferential treatment does not determine the identification of religion but only the deferential treatment itself. The sacred things in various cultures might take ugly or beautiful form, be beneficial or antagonistic toward human beings, look admirable or weird to outside observers. In fact, almost anything we can imagine has been sacred or taboo to some culture or other. The study of religion in this context consists of finding out just what are the holy things for each culture, how they are reverenced, and (often the most difficult task) what is the logic or argument for their selection. The last task can be difficult because religious practices tend to become matters of habit and unreflective obedience so that the reasons that led to their adoption are sometimes lost, and sometimes are accidental even in their origin.

What I shall call the philosophical definition of religion is also based on a bifurcation pattern, but one that is primarily intellectual rather than behavioral. A philosophical definition concentrates on the beliefs or ideas of a religion and tends to analyze those beliefs in light of their demonstrability and their reference to transcendent matters. Insofar as a set of conceptions is based on empirical evidence and logical argument, they are not distinctly religious from this point of view. Those conceptions which are not verifiable, but which are held to be true by people nevertheless, qualify as religious. These matters transcend the ordinary by their optional character.

We have a choice here between a broader or a narrower notion of what is transcendent. The narrower involves belief in spirits, god(s), heaven(s), and the like. These are almost universally agreed to be beyond normal demonstration. However, the broader definition includes ideas about the world and human beings which are not so obviously unempirical. The Buddhist tradition, for example, in its strictest form does not make much of spirits but does define human possibility in a special way. This broad definition could also include Communism with its vision of a transformed humanity in the future, and also various kinds of Humanism. In both forms of the philosophical definition, religion is characterized by a person's belief that something is true which others can very reasonably reject, in that there is no unambiguous or universally convincing proof.

To the precise philosopher's dismay, proof, verification, demonstrability, etc. are matters of degree to many people. In some places and times, more is accepted as proven than at others; and at all times some people are more easily satisfied by rhetorical arguments and suggestive data than are others. Those who think that their religious beliefs are not that much different from all their other ideas in regard to reasonability and general acceptability would not find the philosophical definition reasonable or acceptable, because it assumes a contrast which they do not recognize. At the other extreme there are people who have declared their own and other religions absurd. The practice of calling religions "faiths" supports the notion that religions are precisely those systems that contain concepts one takes on faith, as compared to those one can say one really knows.

In the philosophical kind of definition, religion is the area of things we want to know but cannot. Older religions, by this approach, have been superseded as much by science as by other religions. Nature religions, for example, centered on the mysteries of birth, growth, and reproduction; they dealt in a religious way with matters which have subsequently received rational analysis and treatment. Fertilizers replaced sacrifices; science replaced magic. Many newer religions focused on the mystery of the human psyche and it is now sometimes argued that they too are being replaced by the sciences of psychology, medical chemistry, and eugenics.

In both examples, however, it can also be maintained that despite the advance of technical skill and scientific theory, the essential mysteries are still with us. In those moments when the comforting appearance of human control of the world diminishes we sometimes glimpse the old awe afresh. No matter how much of the mechanics of organic life or the human psyche we may come to know and manipulate, many important questions remain: Where did it all come from? Where is it all going? Why does it all work so well? Why does it not work better, or more to our liking? What is the meaning or significance of all life, human life, and my life? Insofar as religions try to answer these questions, they are not really concerned with the same things sciences investigate and therefore not subject to replacement by them. This is not to say, however, that religious systems, sacred texts, and theologies have not contained replaceable elements. Most intellectual religious systems have attempted to account for many things in addition to the big questions listed above. In so doing such systems have characteristically included descriptions of and propositions about the world which later have been proven wrong to most people's satisfaction, for example a flat earth, the existence of dragons, or a six-day creation.

Certainly much more could be said about the philosophical definition or definitions but we must move on. The next type of approach to religion can be called the "theological" because it appeals to theorists within a religious tradition. It is the kind of definition that fits in best with most of the pieties and meditations of religious people. It is the kind of definition which understands religion to be the term for the area of values, especially important or absolute values. Put in a preacher's terms: Whatever one values most is one's god and the orientation of life to that value is religion. Both individuals and societies as a whole lift up certain symbols and practices for primary allegiance—when push comes to shove these are the things that people think should prevail, whether they actually do or not. When one holds to certain ultimate and absolute values beyond all the other contenders in life, one is religious by this definition.

Obviously the matters so valued will change from culture to culture, individual to individual. A common preacher's assumption is that money or success can become such pre-emptive values in people's lives. Worshippers of these things seem to be short-sighted in their selection of values. It may be wondered, however, whether the devotee of money is any the less religious for having selected a deity which other people demean. It is this definition that produces the oxymoronic expression, "devout atheist," which acknowledges that even opposition to religion or god can have its religious fervor.

There is yet another kind of definition of religion associated with values which relates to the field of ethics. It is observable inside and outside of religious groups. It identifies the distinctively religious with upholding and doing the right thing, as determined by the society at large or the particular sub-group. The right things include right moral actions but also the rituals and etiquette expected of people. In this perspective, being religious is not so much thinking or feeling a certain way but acting, or at least trying to act, according to specific ideals and standards. This is a very ancient notion and was a part of the meaning of the Latin word *religio*.

The ethics definition runs into difficulty when the student observes a religion whose moral ideals differ a great deal from his or her own. Applying the definition requires an extra measure of empathetic imagination in such cases. Religions that practice human sacrifice or cannibalism provide test cases in the use of this definition. The essence of the difficulty is that it takes a lot of effort not to feel some kind of moral repulsion at patterns of action or ideals with which one cannot agree. It has been observed that we generally tolerate differences in ideas more easily than differences in ethical standards and actions.

To be objectively and fairly utilized the ethics definition should be based on the ubiquitous phenomenon that peoples have ethical standards rather than any particular set of ethical standards. No matter how earnestly one agrees with or despises any one ethical value or set. Cannibals might be just as religious by this definition as you or I, even though we would argue against their theology and try to prevent them from practicing their religion. Understanding and tolerance of others' religions are not license to permit all practices. Freedom of religion is appropriately limited when a society prohibits people from exercising their religion when it harms others and perhaps when it harms them themselves. What constitutes harm is, of course, notoriously difficult to determine.

It is possible, of course, to develop an ethics-based definition of religion which is not so tolerant. In such cases some or all religions other than one's own can be judged wrong or evil, even to the point of ascribing them to devils, counter-deities, and the like. It is interesting that a number of people recently have promoted ideas and practices associated with witchcraft as an alternative religion. The argument for this assumes that European witchcraft is the remnant of an old religion condemned as evil by Christianity. Therefore, witchcraft on this approach is not a religion for Christians whose definition of religion includes only religions which are judged to be good, but it may be a religion on the basis of other definitions.

Defining religion in connection with ethical patterns also leads to confusion when the ethical element simply is not as important as one expects it to be. The Western religions, Judaism, Christianity, and Islam, are very much concerned with ethics; for them right behavior is an essential element in one's relationship to one's god. In other religions, however, this element may not be as central. The Western student might, in these circumstances, overestimate the place of ethical standards in such a religion as compared to the role of spiritual disciplines, asceticism, meditation, ritual, and the like. There are a few instances, shocking to many Western students of religions, where the ethical patterns of the surrounding society are deliberately ignored or even flouted in the interests of a ritual or ascetic goal, for example, Left-handed Tantrism in India.

We could continue reviewing the various things people mean when they use the word "religion," but these definitions would become more and more obscure and idiosyncratic. There may be other ways of listing the various meanings, also, but the point about variety should have been made by this time. We would almost be justified in concluding that the word "religion" cannot be used meaningfully at all. Some scholars persist in trying to bring order into the chaos by developing comprehensive definitions but that is a very difficult task. One is forced in such circumstances to voice all sorts of warnings and precautions concerning the word in order to forestall misunderstanding, and misunderstanding often remains after all. People are usually too much wed to their favorite slants and biases to pay much attention to a rival definition of a common word. Successful communication in this case can come about only with constant awareness of the many possibilities involved. When one says the word "religion," one needs always to examine just what one really does mean by it and try to express that in other, ancillary or replacement words. And when one reads or hears "religion," special attention to the context and intention of the author or speaker is essential to avoiding misunderstanding.

The conclusion for which I am arguing is simply that there is no one comprehensive or adequate definition of religion in common usage and there is not likely to be. There is no clear or concise list of the things that might be considered religious. One must take each usage or definition for what it is specifically, that is for what particular thing someone is trying to say by it. Although in a few instances users of "religion" might be outright wrong because they are departing so radically from any of the prevailing meanings, in most instances they will only be selective and partial. They will be right about some aspects or some believers and irrelevant to the others.

This is not to say that the word "religion" is meaningless; the fact is it has too many meanings. There are out there (and in here for that matter) many elements of human behavior, thought, and experience, plus aspects of nature, cultural artifacts, and supernatural beings, which have been called "religious" or "sacred" for good reasons. All of that cannot be dismissed, because it is a firmly established part of the language world we read and hear. Our first task is to ascertain exactly what is being described as religious and why. Beyond that we might ourselves try to be more precise and helpful when we talk about religion with others. That might lead to more cumbersome but more careful sentences. Instead of: "Religion is such-and-such," or "Such-and-such is religious," we will have to say: "According to so-and-so," or "According to this perspective, religion consists of such-and-such."

There are probably a great many items in human life that few people's definitions of religion would exclude, e.g. visions of angels, temples, baptisms, Buddha statues, and ideas about immortality. There are, however, many other items which fall under some definitions and not under others, e.g. Confucianism, initiation rites, Beethoven's Missa Solemnis, emotions at seeing a beautiful sunset, and much more. There are also some things that very few people, if any, would think of as religious. But some of these turn out to have many similarities with the more acceptable examples of religion and are thereby illuminated, e.g. Communism, Fourth of July celebrations, union picket lines, paradigm shifts in the sciences, and other possibilities which seem unlikely at first glance. One might want to call these last kinds of things "pseudo-religious" or "quasi-religious." As always, it would depend on what one took to be real religion to begin with.

It is wise, I think, to reject no definition out of hand. For one thing, it is impossible to control language, the French Academy's attempts to police French notwithstanding. New usages or definitions which gain wide acceptance cannot be dismissed as just plain wrong, but like all the old ones, merely perspectivally specific and therefore limited. It is on such a basis that usage may be criticized modestly and helpfully. "Religion" means neither everything nor nothing. It can mean many interesting things, interesting conceptions about what human beings are and do. It is worth the trouble to get behind the word in each instance to examine the conjectures and constructions it represents.

3 | THE OLD RELIGIONS

Just as the word "religion" is not a simple label that can be assigned to specific things, so the names of the religions are not as obvious as we might expect. There are some fairly well-defined religious groups which have official names (The Society of Friends, Brahmo Samaj, etc.). These and other fairly small groups can be defined by reference to the individuals who are members, the writings and practices which are observed, and other predominant features. Things become much more difficult the larger and longer the tradition which one is trying to classify or name.

Also, we face the common problem of a possible difference of opinion and usage between believers and outside observers. Believers are prone to make theological assertions with the names that they use of themselves and their tradition, e.g. they may consider themselves the only Christians, while many other people think they are Christian too. Drawing the boundaries, deciding who and what are in or out of the particular religion, is the biggest source of trouble in the definitions of the various religions' names. We also notice that outside observers often give names to religious groups or traditions, which their adherents may or may not like (e.g. calling the Friends "Quakers"). It may even be the case that the believers or members of what we want to identify as a religious group may not even think of themselves as members of a religion, let alone know what its name is.

In order to survey some of the words for various religions, a division will made between the primitive and most ancient cultures discussed in this chapter, and, in the next chapter, later religious groups. First we must turn our attention to words for the human cultures which seem to be the simplest and most basic.

The term "primitive" is applied widely to certain kinds of cultures and their religions but it implies some questionable things about such cultures. When you try merely to identify, without prejudice, a type of religion, some other associations of the word used may lurk in the background. Primitive is derived from the Latin for first or earliest, and it thus promotes the theory that such cultures, even as they are observed today, are identical to or very much like the earliest human society. Primitive is also used, for example in grammatical studies, to mean something not derived from something else and therefore basic and primary. It may or may not be the case, however, that the societies which have been called "primitive" over the years really are either representative of the first stage of human society or the basic form of it. These cultures have had their history too and may have changed in all sorts of ways so that their resemblance to any prehistoric state of humankind would be purely accidental. There is in many people so strong a desire to know the origins of humanity and religion that the supposition of relic societies from the past is very attractive and names like "primitive" presuppose a way to know this remote human past.

Primitive, however, has become a pejorative term in addition to having theoretical assumptions. If one adopts the belief that progress is the good and proper process of human history, and that this progress is to be measured in terms of complexity, technology, power, and the like, then the primitive peoples are at best retarded and at worst sub-human or culturally sick. When this kind of attitude is involved in the use of primitive, one is not just identifying or even describing such cultures but also judging them. This judging is a practice which should be exercised gingerly and consciously, if at all, in the study of other peoples. There is much to be said in appreciation and respect for the so-called primitive societies. No matter what the terminology, closer study can be expected to produce for some people a reverse judgment, namely that many technologically simple cultures have extraordinary beauty and depth.

At least "primitive" is better than "savage," which is derived from words meaning forest and cognate with words like sylvan. Savage implies that such people are like animals and this idea can be used to condone treating them similarly. A lot of this attitude can be blamed on sensationalist reporting. From the days of early explorers' reports to the present, it has been more entertaining to describe the odd and horrible features of foreign peoples. The ways in which they seem to be most unusual arrests our attention more than affirming their similarity to us. Their religious or symbolic practices can be expected to be more odd than their normal pursuits. In addition to being entertaining and instead of evoking bemused horror or colonial enterprise, explorers' reports have also inspired good-hearted missionary enterprise and sincere charitable work. The implication remains in all these responses, however, that such peoples must be improved, humanized, and civilized; that is, changed into something else which is better.

Anthropologists and others who wish to discard all such programs and to understand these cultures in and of themselves, with as little insidious comparison and judgment as possible, have sought other, less tainted, terms by which to name primitive cultures. Primal, primary, and primordial are words which avoid some of the emotion but none of the theoretical assumptions. "Aborigine" has the same etymological structure and implication but also some of the same condescending tone as primitive. "Aboriginal" tends to be used especially for small hunting and gathering bands. "Tribal" can be used of all these cultures or for those which have somewhat larger social units than the wandering bands. "Pre-literate" focuses on an incidental common factor by which to classify such cultures, but, of course, if one prizes literacy one is at least sorry for those who lack it. "Peripheral" concentrates on a peripheral characteristic, that is, being geographically remote from the centers of civilization.

No commonly used word entirely removes the possibility of demeaning or speculative connotations, so we may be forced to use an old word, like primitive, after all. It is somewhat ironic that there is a positive meaning of primitive in English in its use by some religious groups to emphasize their adherence to the basic, original Christian teachings, e.g., "Primitive Methodists." The irony lies in this expressed desire to be what some would take to be backward or ancient in the face of the prevailing modern emphases on progress and advancement. In less specifically religious circles there is another positive type of approach to the meaning of primitive, the idea of the noble savage whom civilization corrupts.

We may conclude that religious people and students of religions take different positions about the origins of humanity, depending on their scheme of historical change, whether it is pictured as progress or decline. Whether one desires an antiseptic, value-free classification or a more value-laden term, primitive and its synonyms will have to be qualified and explained to avoid unwanted connotations.

Another word used in connection with the cultures called primitive is "animism." It was popularized by Edward Tylor, an English anthropologist of the nineteenth century. It is sometimes used today to name the religion of primitive peoples, even by people who do not subscribe to Tylor's specific theories. For him the basic form of religion was a belief in spirit persons, immaterial personal souls. He went to the Latin-Greek word *anima* for a word not associated with Christian views of the soul with which it might otherwise be confused. If used in Tylor's sense, one is making an analytical statement about the content and basic convictions of primitive religious systems. His contemporaries and subsequent readers were quick to argue that not all, if any, actual primitive religions held the animistic doctrine that Tylor formulated. If all the religiosity of primitive peoples is still called animism it must be in the loosest and most casual sense, a move of despair since there is no other-ism to use on maps or in outlines. The conceptions of spirit, soul, and similar words upon which Tylor's theories were based will be discussed later.

One of the objections to the animistic theory of primitive religion was based on the observation that many of the powers or taboos observed by primitive peoples seem to be impersonal, conceived in terms of forces which act automatically. This led to the term "pre-animism." The Melanesian word *mana* was widely used in explaining this kind of belief. *Mana* seems to have been for the Melanesian people an impersonal potency found in certain things, places, or people, which had to be treated in a special way. Admitting the idea of *mana* pushed the origin of religion back beyond animism. For some theorists, however, the admission of the impersonal conception of the powers of the universe removed a system of belief from the realm of religion and moved into the sphere of magic.

Something must be said about the use of "magic," in reference to both the modern and primitive worlds. Here another nineteenth century Englishman has been very influential. James George Frazer (most famous for *The Golden Bough*) theorized that religion should be used of only some primitive practices and beliefs, because he restricted that word to situations in which a deity of some sort was addressed and served. As he read travelers' accounts of various exotic peoples and as he examined ancient texts, it seemed to him that many primitive activities and observances did not have this interpersonal character, but they were also not quite practical or scientific either. The activities connected with non-scientific beliefs in powers and processes which were impersonal in character, he called magic rather than religion.

Frazer had a somewhat positive view of primitive magic. He saw magical activity as a means of dealing with the world in a more responsible and rational way than religion does. He assumed that humankind probably developed magical practices and depended on them for a while before resorting, in despair, to prayer and sacrifice as a way of getting help in facing difficulties. Magic, from this point of view, was more like science than religion, except that its procedures were based on faulty assumptions, such as the principles of sympathy, contagion, and imitation. Other scholars, however, have theorized that it is as likely if not more so, that an original religious sense deteriorated into crass magic rather than the reverse. Insofar as this is a debate about prehistoric developments for which there can be only ambiguous evidence, one cannot expect it to be settled. Until the stage for which we have written records, we cannot be sure about anything concerning thoughts and ideas in human history. Analysis of pre-history is a matter of theorizing from archeological evidence and that tells us little about human minds. Evidence from contemporary primitive and literate religions is ambiguous enough that it can be used to support either of these views, the priority of magic or religion.

It might seem, on first glance, that it would be easy to define magic in terms of characteristic acts or effects, but that turns out to be very difficult, like the identification of what is miraculous. Instead, some scholarship sees the main defining characteristic of magic in the attempt to affect or manipulate the world by means of prescribed acts and words. Thus magic is defined in terms of a certain attitude or intention in the mind of a person doing a ritual act. Some ritual activities do not seem to need this kind of analysis, spontaneous prayer for example; but almost all other ceremonials or chants can be considered magical if the commentator thinks that the actor's or speaker's attitude is one of manipulative intent. Since attitudes are private, the charge of magic can be misused easily. By this definition any ritual act that is held to change something in and of itself (*ex opere operato*), for example a blessing, ordination, or sacrifice, can be termed magical.

It is difficult to avoid the negative connotations of magic, even if the observer wants to use the word only to describe or name a kind of belief or act. Certainly much of the ritual activity of religions is in this way linked with the connotations of magic as foolish or evil activity. Magic may be positive in the world of entertainment today, but in religion it has usually had a bad reputation. The ancient Greeks apparently associated the practice of magic (possibly with the overtone of charlatanism) with the Persian hereditary priesthood, the Magi. Thus it is an ancient prejudice that magic is what other religions do and it is not respectable. Neither the intent to manipulate the world or the depersonalization of religion have been approved by Western religions. The condemnation of such characteristics is expressed when these elements in other cultures and religions are called magic. This word, even more than others in this chapter, may be so polluted with unwanted associations that it will have to be completely avoided.

When primitive, animism, and to a great extent magic, are used in the study of religion they refer to the very small, relatively undifferentiated tribal societies on the periphery of the modern world. Today there is little in the religious scene other than these fast-disappearing cultures plus the major-isms that we will discuss in the next chapter. Historically, however, there have been religions and cultures that do not quite fit in either category. There were some peoples in the distant past whose societies were more complex and whose religions and cultures were more elaborate than seem to fit into most conceptions of primitive, but they have been replaced by newer forms, i.e. the major modern religions. These ancient cultures begin to appear in what is called the Neolithic period, the new stone age, which is apparent in the Near East by 5000 BCE. (I shall use the date indicator BCE, before the common era in this book rather than the culturally-biased BC, before Christ). The difference between these new cultures and what preceded them (which was possibly like the primitive societies left in existence today) was so great that some have called this change the Neolithic revolution.

We are faced here with a terminological problem the reverse of what we usually face; instead of one word with many meanings, we have one meaning with many words. We need a name for the ancient civilizations of the Near East, the Indus river valley, the

Khmer at Angkor, ancient Java, China, and Meso-America. Most of these civilizations have been replaced or radically changed, especially since about 500 BCE, but texts, arts, and ideas from these cultures continue to be well-known and influential. Elements of these cultures are usually studied in connection with their successor cultures and religions, but it is also useful to examine them and give them a name as a group.

Because of their complexity and technology, they have been called civilizations, in contrast to their predecessors. These are the societies which developed field agriculture to the point where it could sustain large populations in relatively small areas. The phenomenon of the state appeared as a specifically political organization. The efforts of individuals became more specialized, interdependent, or differentiated. Relatively permanent buildings and cities were constructed. And, most important for the study of religion and culture, writing was invented. With written records history begins, everything previous being consigned to the category pre-history.

Again, we have the problem of built-in prejudice in the use of "civilization" if that demeans all previous or otherwise structured societies. All human societies have some kind of civil life, socially transmitted patterns of culture. Thus, in a broad sense all peoples are by being human also in some sense civilized. Nevertheless, we also have this narrower meaning of civilization which is based on the special characteristics that emerge with the Neolithic cultures. These cultures may seem more worthy to be called civilizations because of the complexity of their social organization and their literacy.

The ancient civilizations are sometimes differentiated from later or other civilizations by being called archaic. This word has a number of dimensions, most of which are involved in this application. The basic meaning of *arche* in Greek is first, beginning, origin, and "archaic" retains elements of that sense. These cultures called archaic are first in many things. There is also a sense in the related Greek word *archaios* of something that is old-fashioned and obsolete. Archaic, in dictionary terminology indicates words which are not common in contemporary speech, used, if at all, to give a flavor of bygone eras. Thus, these cultures are archaic by being first at so much and also in being obsolete. They have all been superseded by different civilizations and religions. There is a third aspect of archaic, however, which takes first to mean primary and basic, as is also implied in some uses of primitive." In this last sense archaic is like the related term "archetype" in referring to something that persists in human life, from the beginning to the present. Many of the elements of these ancient civilizations do remain with us as major cultural hallmarks, even if in changed form.

This third dimension of archaic is not prominent in English usage. The idea of the ancient cultures also providing perennial aspects of human life is more obviously expressed by calling them "classical." Most specifically it is the Greek and Roman cultures that have been the classical cultures for the Western world. In some contexts classical simply refers to the texts, art, and other remains of these two ancient civilizations. Classical is also used to mean that which constitutes a standard for its type, the highest class or first rank. In their respective cultural traditions many of the ancient cultures have classical status, that is, prestige as well as priority. Of course, more recent cultural materials also have become classics in their traditions. Popular and respected writings or other cultural artifacts sometimes attain to such widespread prominence that they become the major symbolic representatives of the contexts out of which they emerged and of the cultures which they continue to influence. This meaning of classical, however, has taken us beyond the ancient civilizations which we have been trying to name.

Something should be said here concerning some very influential cultures which do not fit into the category of the ancient civilizations and yet affected them deeply in some instances. These are the cattle and sheep herders collectively called "pastoralists." Some African pastoralist cultures (e.g., the Nuer and Dinka) are studied in connection with the primitive cultures. Many primitive peoples were wandering hunters and gatherers, but the groups that depended on large animal herds are distinguishable from the rest. The most ancient Indo-Europeans and the Hebrews were pastoralists, and, by invading some archaic civilizations and blending with them, they created a set of important cultures. They adopted the technology of the agriculturally based societies they invaded and produced cultural phenomena which they could not have had as long as they were mobile. The worldview of these pastoralists was different from the agriculturalist civilizations and that difference is reflected in the ancient texts they produced. The Hebrew Bible is the result of one pastoralist group's experience. The Indo-Europeans' experiences are reflected in the Vedic literature in India as well as parts of the Persian, Greek, and Roman traditions.

The differences between the religions of the pastoralists and the agriculturally based archaic civilizations largely grew out of their different sources of food, and consequently different lifestyles. The agriculturalist was dependent on the fertility of a certain stretch of land. Much of their ancient religiosity was therefore concerned with symbols of sexuality, growth, and harvest, in the fervent hope that this limited land resource would sustain human life. Women as the nurturers of human birth and growth were reflected symbolically in the agriculturalist emphasis on goddesses and mother figures. These religions are sometimes called "fertility religions" because of their emphasis on generation and growth. The pastoralists, by contrast, tended to emphasize male gods associated with the sky and aerial phenomena, without as much reference to sexual matters or symbolism.

The symbolism of all the ancient and primitive religions is derived to a great extent from the natural world, but the same could be said of much symbolism of all times and places. The agriculturalist societies, however, are deliberately and constantly focused on nature in a way in which the others are not. The other religions often use a natural phenomenon as a metaphor for something not immediately associated with the physical world. By contrast, real rain, fertility, and food production are the concern of agricultural religiosity. Because of their intense involvement with natural processes the agriculturalist religions are sometimes called "nature religions." That term necessitates further consideration of the word "nature."

The Latin *natura* is linked to the word for birth, as indicated by other English words, e.g. nativity. Thus nature is at root a word for the organic, the animal, and the reproductive aspects of life. The Greek *physis* has similar etymology but has developed in English a closer association with the non-organic aspects of the world. It is in this root sense of birth, despite many other ramifications, that nature is appropriate to those cultures and religions for which the phenomenon of sexual reproduction was the dominant set of symbols by which to understand the world.

There are other meanings of nature which are not as relevant to the immediate problem of naming ancient religions, but which are important in other contexts. In something of an excursus let us consider those other meanings here. Nature, as often used today, refers to the realm of plants, animals, and the physical world, all that is visible or phenomenal as distinguished from the supernatural or the abstract. This nature, in contemporary thought, is understood to be governed by scientifically discoverable laws and processes. It is important to recognize that the cluster of modern associations with nature is not necessarily shared by non-modern cultures. Obviously, nature for a nature religion is not scientifically described; it contains characteristics which the modern mind would relegate to the realm of human projection and imagination.

The word miracle helps to explain the distinction between usages of the word nature. To a modern mind a miracle is something that happens contrary to the laws of nature. The word "miracle" derives, however, from a Latin word best translated by words like wonder. This indicates that older, pre-modern worldviews might admit that some events are amazing and extraordinary but without the hard line demarcating what is possible and impossible according to natural laws. So if we say that a religion is concerned with nature or that it treasures stories of miracles we should not assume that all the assumptions about nature which modern people have are involved in the ancient view. Miracles may or may not be supernatural, depending on one's definition of nature.

Nature is also used to refer to the essential quality, character, or temperament of something or someone. This notion carries with it the idea that such items are given, essential, and unchangeable—what a thing must be to be that thing at all. Of course, this is related to the idea of birth in that such nature is present at the beginning and remains throughout a thing's existence; it is not added later, even in those cases where it does not appear immediately. In this context each thing, person, species, or anything else has its own nature. In many theological systems it is important to define the true nature of things, especially true human nature, for from that definition all sorts of implications for ethics and salvation flow. In many Christian theologies, for example, human nature is not natural because it is a fallen nature, incapable of being true to its true nature.

To return to primitive religions, it is important to take note of that meaning of nature understood as an alternative to culture. In this context nature is the non-human world plus some aspects of human beings. Human beings are often understood to be at the same time parts and products of nature, and yet also self-made, and makers in turn of another kind of thing, the artificial or the cultural. It would seem that the perception of the nature/culture distinction was very important to many primitive cultures and that it still influences human thought. This is interestingly described as the distinction between the raw and the cooked, that is, what the world gives in contrast with the changes human beings make. Much controversy, both inside and outside of religious groups, can be reduced to the question of whether human beings improve on nature or corrupt it. The noble savage theory took the latter view while many others take the former or a mix of the two.

At a more informal level, nature and natural are used to designate the normal or the acceptable, and unnatural is a word of rejection and criticism. Such a judgment is dependent on the culturally accepted notions of just what is natural in the issue at hand. Of course, people using nature in this sense do not think that they are acting on cultural prejudice. They assume that their judgments are based on some more or less consistent notion of what is natural, from which certain things, acts, forms, and so on can depart. These notions about what is natural, and what various kinds of departure from it (supernatural or subnatural) mean, are an important part of a people's worldview and religion. In summary, nature can refer to the physical world, especially the organic world, or to the non-human world. It can indicate an arena of strict laws and processes or an open-ended realm of possibilities. It can be a word of commendation or censure. Obviously, this is a word of which to be wary.

With this summary of the meanings of nature and its use to describe the content of some ancient religions we come to the end of the terms to be discussed in connection with primitive and archaic religions. It is a handy stopping point because the next group of religions is usually discussed with different words. This indicates a consensus that they are as a group significantly different from the kinds of religions and cultures we have categorized and named so far.

4 | THE NEW RELIGIONS

Saying that the previous section was about old and this one about new religions, is itself controversial, but less so than some other terminology. Every time such a large category is named there are bound to be hidden assumptions and presumptions about the material designated. At least it is generally assumed that the conceptions which were summarized in the previous chapter deal with human religion practically since its beginnings or since the prehistoric Neolithic revolution. The following matters are dateable, no more than three millennia old.

Some would use the term "modern" for the period of new religions that begins around the middle of the last millennium BCE, but it is more usual to reserve that word for later developments. The word "historic" has been used, to indicate that these new religious developments occur within the scope of historical records. There are also sociological and political bases for identifying and naming the contrast with the old religions. The primitive and archaic religions and cultures were local and/or national, limited to particular ethnic groups or geographical areas. The religions we are trying to categorize now usually transcend these boundaries, sooner or later, and can be called "international" or "universal" religions. All these terms, modern, historic, and universal, deserve more analysis and it will be given them later, but there are yet other terms that have been used for the new religions that are not as complex, but still problematic.

Some people want to call these the "living" religions because many of them are still in existence. One, however, is not as prominent as it once was, Zoroastrianism. Also living involves changing and these religions are certainly living in a different way now than they were in their infancies. Some people have named these the "high" or "higher" religions, and that is obviously a value judgment. Certainly these religions are later than some others, although even this can be disputed by certain believers who believe, despite historical evidence, that contemporary beliefs are primordial in origin. In any event, later is not used much, while high or higher clearly implies gradation, perhaps an evolutionary schema, or a scale of importance. If one wishes to use such terms, one should at least be aware that judgments are implicit and need to be made explicit at some point. "Higher" might mean that these religions are more complex, more subtle or elaborate in thought, social structure, and ritual, also more complex because of internal divisions and varieties. In religion, however, these may not be positive values, and it is as easy from other points of view to see these as the lower religions by contrast with the virtues of their predecessors or alternatives.

We can date the shift from the older to the newer religions at around 500 BCE. During the few hundred years around this date the archaic religions underwent great changes and experienced the development of new traditions or religions in their midst. These few centuries contain a disproportionate number of the great names in the history of religions. Karl Jaspers called this the Axial Age and dated it from 800 to 200 BCE. Within this period we find the Hebrew literary prophets, the authors of the major Upanishads of Hinduism, Confucius and Lao-tze in China, Zoroaster in Persia, Mahavira of the Jain religion and Gautama Buddha in India, and Socrates, Plato, et al. in Greece. Some writers stretch the axial period so that it includes Jesus and even Mohammed, but this adds another 200 or 800 years and diminishes the impressiveness of so much happening in so short a time.

In order to review the names of the prominent religions which arose out of the axial period and later, it is illuminating to reverse the chronological order and begin with the latest of the very large traditions, Islam. Unlike most other religions this one named itself and thus alerts us to an interesting phenomenon in the language of religion studies, that religions are usually named by outsiders. Islam was also given a name by some outsiders, "Mohammedanism." This name can be offensive to Muslims, even though the offense may not have been intended. This unfortunate naming may be due to Western language users, including users of English, being over-impressed with one characteristic of historic religions, their origin in the work of a teacher, preacher, or founder. Therefore, the pattern prevailed of calling the teachings and adherents of such teachings after the founder, e.g. "Confucianism," "Zoroastrianism," "Buddhism."

Seen in this light Mohammedanism does not seem strange. Many Muslims, however, see in this a subtle put-down of their religion; this naming seems to say that Islam is not able to speak for itself about itself but must be subject to the interpretive words and categories of others. Of course, it is inevitably the case that outsiders will use their own terminology and interpretive patterns to comprehend whatever they can of a foreign phenomenon, but it is especially irritating when the foreign category or terminology is unnecessary. There is a perfectly good name for this religion, "Islam," and its adherents are "Muslims." Why use other words? Also, it is sometimes maintained that use of the Mohammedanism implies a greater role or position for Mohammed than is theologically acceptable in Islam. In contradistinction to Christianity, Muslims have been clear in denying divinity to their founder, no matter how much he is to be respected as the last prophet.

There is an important issue involved in the very naming of a religion. A name which identifies a particular religion might be understood to imply that this religion is just one example of the larger category, religion. Such an assumption is in itself offensive to the beliefs of a great many religious people, because people characteristically affirm a religion as the truth, the only way to live properly, the correct picture of the world. Other religions or viewpoints are wrong, stupid, diabolical, or at least incomplete. From such a position one does not name one's own religion as if it were one position among many. It is only necessary on occasion to name the heresies, the mistakes and delusions, from which believers should be defended. Naming has been, therefore, often a means of repudiating a religion, not of affirming it.

Only in the last few centuries has the existence of many religious affiliations within one society become common enough for the reluctant admission of religious particularity to enter into language. As consciousness of pluralism has become more widespread, both believers (and opposers) of religions, plus the early academic students of religions, increasingly have named the various traditions as well as their own. They have used various-isms and other constructions. Even where the name-words themselves were much older, their use to denominate a body of teachings, practices, peoples, and texts has increased dramatically under the pressure of the pluralistic situation.

It is not surprising, therefore, that some religious groups do not like the name outsiders gave them. Some religions did not even recognize that they were any such thing. Other believers, as in the case of Islam, resented the assumptions made about their religion by the outsiders' name and its presuppositions. Some groups, however, ended up adopting and cherishing the name the outsiders gave them. This might well be the origin of the name "Christian," which in its Greek origin may have been a word of derision, meaning something like oily one.

The essential contrast is not, however, between complimentary and insulting terminology but between the view of a religion which its believers have and that which observers have. While some people try to see themselves as others see them, an attempt I applaud, this is not common. Thus the cleavage in terminology: One's own religion is faith, obedience, the way, the way of the gods, or simply religion, as if there is only one. Other religions, meanwhile, are the "isms" which the observer constructs in the process of trying to understand other peoples' ideas, practices, and texts.

While the study of religions must respect the beliefs and wishes of religious people as much as possible, it cannot be limited to their words and categories. There are many things which an outsider can and should say about a religious community and its component aspects which may be difficult or impossible to recognize from the inside. These things may or may not be distressing for the believers to take into consideration. Especially embarrassing is the extent to which the actual behavior of the community does not live up to its ideals. It is also irritating to be put into a large category where the special dynamics of a particular group are lost in the magnitude of the generalization. All these things are understandable and in some sense regrettable, but if the study of religion is worth doing at all, it is worthwhile to make generalizations and categorizations at many levels. This is legitimate as long as it is also clear that these categories are gross and inexact apprehensions, always in need of refinement and adjustment.

With these factors in mind we can understand not only the Muslim's rejection of Mohammedanism but a difference between the Muslim use of Islam and the use of the same word by the student of religions. For the latter, Islam is primarily the name of a religion, that is, of a set of beliefs and practices. For the Muslim it refers to the central attitudes and acts of his or her religious life. Islam for the Muslim means submission of one's will to God, obeisance, self-surrender. It is the heart of his or her piety to act and feel the posture of total subjection of self before Allah, and thus the worshipper is called a Muslim, one who submits to God.

Islam almost always appears with this spelling. Many words used by Muslims and used of Islamic things are originally Arabic words, or words from other languages in the Islamic world. This brings up the phenomenon of transliteration, an issue which deserves some attention before we proceed to a consideration of the rest of the terminology for the major religions. Whenever a word from another language begins to be used in English without translation, that is, becomes an English word, decisions are made regarding the degree to which the word will preserve the characteristics of its original language or become anglicized. Transliteration requires finding the spelling and pronunciation that is close to the foreign original while still using standard elements of English writing. Even closely related languages present this problem: For example the German umlaut is now usually converted to English spelling by adding an "e" after the letter that bore the umlaut but in former years other devices were used, thus "muller" could become "miller" or "mueller." Transliteration is much more difficult when the original language uses a different alphabet or an even more different way of writing language, e.g. Chinese characters.

Standard patterns for the transliteration of each language are becoming accepted in English publications today, especially for those words that have not had a history of English usage but are being newly incorporated into English texts. These transliteration systems usually try to reproduce the features of the original language by introducing extra symbols. These may be symbols which are not used in traditional English or not used in the same way, but might be available on computer keyboards. Thus dots, apostrophes, dashes, etc., will be used in effect to expand the English alphabet and introduce finer discriminations and different sounds than are inherent in it. At the same time one finds books published in former years which reflect various other ways of solving the transliteration problem and one must exercise a certain imagination in deciphering the old spellings.

"Muslim" can be found in old books as "Moslem" and "Mussulman." The situation can be confusing, for example, in the name of the sacred revelation in Islam. It is now usually transliterated "Qur'an," but it has formerly been "Koran." "Muhammad," the prophet of Islam, can appear as "Mohammed," "Mohamet," and a few other similar forms.

Having reviewed the problems of religion-naming and transliteration in connection with Islam it will be a little easier to discuss the names of the other religions. We meet up with other kinds of problems, however. One is the issue of the appropriateness of different names for different periods in a long religious tradition. This is illustrated in the Hebrew-Jewish situation. This religion or series of religions, depending on one's solution to this problem, is over three thousand years old. It is not, given that observation, surprising that it has changed quite a bit over the years. It is possible, of course, to emphasize the continuity and the similarity in all that time; this is often the emphasis of the believer. It is also possible to focus on the differences from one period to another, and the historian or outsider may be more interested in that. In the case of the Hebrew-Jewish tradition, however, there are political and geographical factors that aid in making distinctions between the periods, stages, or religions within the whole tradition.

The word "Hebrew" can be used to refer to the language and the earliest historical form of this tradition. Emerging out of the pastoralist peoples of the Near East a group of tribes settled in the lower Eastern Mediterranean region. The Hebrew name may have come from a Semitic word for wandering people. Being the first word for the tradition and for its language, Hebrew continues to be used as a name for the whole tradition. The Hebrew settlers, however, had another name for their tribal confederation, "Israel." This names their corporate identity during their pre-monarchial period and their short (less than a century) existence as a monarchy under the kings: Saul, David, and Solomon. When this kingdom split into two, the northern section retained the name Israel and the southern part took the name of its dominant tribe, Judah. During this period, the first half of the millennium BCE, the united Israel, then (northern) Israel, and Judah all seem to have shared a more or less common religion and culture which can be called ancient Israelite religion. To confuse the use of Israel further, we should add, out of chronological order, that it is also the name of the contemporary nation in that same area.

During the axial period, the Israelite tradition underwent significant transformation. The northern kingdom, Israel, was defeated and fades from the scene. Later, Judah too was conquered and its religious practices were affected by the new historical situation. By the time the vassal kingdom of Judah was being reconstructed, around 500 BCE, a number of significant changes had begun to take place. This was due to the political trauma plus the way in which Judah's preachers, the prophets, interpreted those events and reinterpreted the symbols and ideas of the tradition. Some tried to re-instate the ancient Israelite religious practice and theology in the Judah of 500 BCE. Others, however, began to develop a new kind of practice and theology, an axial age version of the tradition. The new version is often called "Judaism" even though the tribe and then the kingdom of Judah had existed long before. "Jew" and its compounds are derived from "Judah."

Judaism can be understood summarily as the Israelite or Hebrew religion forced to live without its temple and national identity. The temple did not exist during much of the sixth century BCE and many of the adherents of the tradition increasingly lived elsewhere far from Judah. In both cases, the temple could not be the actual center of religious life. Instead of priests and sacrifices, teachers and texts began to dominate the piety and theology of this emerging new kind of religion. Under other governments and rulers, the national identity became more what we would call "ethnic" identity. Luckily for the tradition, that transition could take place gradually over about five centuries before the temple in Jerusalem was destroyed again, making the central practices of the old religion impossible ever since.

Confusion occurs when many people use Judaism to mean the whole tradition starting with the most ancient Hebrew beginnings. Certainly the old texts are still read even though regulations for the temple and its rituals are at least temporarily irrelevant.

We could go further in our word-study of this tradition (as we could have done also with Islam) and examine the terminology for the sub-divisions of and outgrowths from the tradition. That would involve us in a much longer project than is appropriate here. It is also (as is just about everything else in the study of religions) controversial. As religious traditions change and grow, believers and outside observers both must make category choices. When is the change so great that the new is no longer to be considered part of the old?

The groups which develop somewhat separate ideas and practices, and yet exhibit some of the features of the predecessor or larger tradition, can be understood as separate religions, as heresies, or as internal variations. It is a matter of where one chooses to draw the line. To use some Islamic examples: Are the Druze to be considered Muslims or members of a separate, if related, religion? How does one classify the Bahai movement? American "black" Muslims have been sorting out their relationships with the rest of Islam over the last few decades. A deeper study of any culture and religion involves careful examination of these decisions and the terminology that reflects them. At this level of investigation we are dealing only with the largest and least exact of the categories and names.

We have already noted the origin of the word Christian in Greek. The early members of the movement talked about their founder as the messiah of the Hebrew-Jewish tradition, and the Hebrew term messiah referred to an anointed one. Therefore they gave him a title in Greek, *christos*, which also meant something like anointed, oiled or salved. Whether it was at first a joke or not, the name Christian stuck; after all, it was appropriate, given the importance of messianic symbolism in the theology of the new movement.

The names for the major groupings within Christianity need some explanation. One strain of Judaism is called "orthodox"; so is one branch of Christianity. It is the Eastern part, that is East of Rome, mainly the Greek and Russian Churches, plus all the other groups which relate loosely to the patriarch of Constantinople (Istanbul). Another major segment is commonly called "Catholic" and consists of the Christians who recognize the bishop of Rome, or the pope, as their leader. Catholic also means universal, however, and is so used in creeds and other theological language by people who are not Catholics in the other sense of the term. "Protestant" is used to designate almost everything else and encompasses thousands of Christian groups which have appeared since the sixteenth century. The name derives from the rejection, in part or whole, of Roman Catholic doctrine, practice, and authority by some people during that century. It is also applied to further divisions and rejections within that tradition ever since. Protest and reform are key concepts in this large category of Christian churches but little else is common to all of them. Many books would be necessary to sort, name, and characterize them all.

The three religions we have mentioned so far are related to each other and reflect in their development the kind of category decisions upon which we were just reflecting. It was a matter of debate within the Christian movement at first, whether this was a new form of Judaism or a more radical departure, a new religion despite its clearly Jewish background. Likewise, Islam sees itself as the continuation and culmination of what was happening in the Jewish and Christian traditions, although again with reinterpretation of the former elements. Interesting in this regard is the incorporation of the older religion's texts into the Christian Bible as the Old Testament, a very obvious indication of connection, compared with Islam's complete replacement of Jewish and Christian texts with the Qur'an. I shall not give any more attention at this point to the many terms in English derived from Christianity. Many of them come up in the context of the naming of religious phenomena reviewed in other chapters.

Leaving the religions that grew out of the Near East, and skipping Greece and Persia where the terminology is not as confusing, we come to India where a number of religions and words deserve our attention. "Hinduism" is clearly a word invented by outside observers. It is questionable whether it names one religion or a number of religions. It can be defined as vaguely as the religious and social system native to India, thus including everything except the obvious alien traditions, like Islam, and perhaps the obvious departures, like Buddhism. Even in these instances, however, the divisions are blurred at the edges. India has been so very creative religiously that it has both produced much variety from within and adopted much from without, making categorization risky.

India and Hindu with all their variations are derived ultimately from the name of a river, the Indus, in what is now Pakistan. The Muslims named everything around and beyond the Indus to the East using the Persian word hindu. For them it meant everything there which was native, that is, not Muslim. However, the origin some of that apparently native tradition was itself foreign. The earliest religious literature of India, the Vedas, were composed by a people who were self-conscious about being invaders and conquerors, the Aryans. They were an Indo-European group which probably brought much of what later became Hinduism with them from Central Asia. The word "Aryan" has acquired some unfortunate connotations by its use in Nazi Germany for the supposed pure German race. The Nazis took it from scholarship on Indo-European cultures which sometimes used it to name the original parent language of this group. In Sanskrit it means noble, and is used in Sanskrit texts without specific cultural or ethnic implications.

Certainly the Indian Aryans were influenced by the peoples they conquered and among whom they settled, but the nature and extent of that influence is much debated. The Indus Valley culture that existed before the Aryan invasion, called also the "Harappan civilization," cannot be very well known as long as its language is undeciphered, and even then we would not know about other non-Aryan peoples in ancient India. The religion reflected in the Vedic texts is assumed to be some mix of Aryan with Harappan background and constitutes the first historical religion in India, in existence by 1000 BCE. As elsewhere, the axial period produced a number of changes. The Upanishad texts in India represent the transformation of the old religion, Vedism, Brahminism or simply the ancient Indian religion, into Hinduism. Here again we face the possibility that many Hindus and others would include the Vedic period within Hinduism. But it can also be understood as a separate religion or stage of development. The Vedas themselves are chanted in the ritual practice of Hinduism but it is questionable whether they are used or understood in the same ways in which they were before the axial period.

At the same time that the Upanishads were re-interpreting the Vedic tradition, there were religious teachers in India with more radical ideas—radical at least in the sense that they involved, eventually, a greater departure from the terms and symbols of the Vedas. There were many of these teachers but the two whose influence has persisted until today were Vardhamana, also called Mahavira, the founder of Jainism; and Siddhartha Gautama, also called the Buddha, founder of Buddhism. Because Jainism and Buddhism as movements and as bodies of teachings were self-conscious and specific departures from the Vedic religion and from other movements emerging in the axial period in India, they have tended to have greater definition and clarity as separate religions both then and now. Buddhism has a little less of this definitional clarity than Jainism, because it has been a much larger movement and has traveled to and been adapted by many cultures outside India. Hinduism, meanwhile, remains a kind of leftover term—whatever is not something else in India is Hindu.

Many quite different styles of religious activity and thought are placed in this loose category, Hinduism, but this category is not entirely a foreign imposition. There are some common features which would pretty well characterize all that goes by the name, and these features of commonality are also affirmed in various ways by Hindus themselves. For example, there are prominent deities in the tradition, like Vishnu and Shiva which are almost always a part of any Hindu system, even though they will be variously ranked, worshipped, and conceptualized, depending on the particular subdivision involved. Respect for the Vedic texts also provides a defining characteristic. Third, an ability to incorporate new and foreign religions into its life and thought is itself a hallmark of Hinduism in most of its forms. Muhammad and Jesus are readily revered as teachers or deities by Hindus. No wonder then that a tradition with this kind of protean syncretism gives pigeon-holers nightmares. It does no good to insist that a religion or a tradition be something other than it is in order to fit into one's categories; the categories and their use must adjust instead to whatever anomalous or random state of affairs humankind presents to us.

China challenges us with yet different problems in religious nomenclature. All the religions we have discussed so far, even Hinduism eventually if not at first, developed organizational and institutional identity, especially when and as they were brought into contact with other groups by contrast with whom they recognized their particularity. The Chinese do not seem to have felt this need. The religious affiliations of China are more fluid, and so depart from the sociological expectations one might bring from other cultures. There are no words in Chinese which would identify someone as a Confucian, Taoist, or even Buddhist. One person can at various times and in various ways be all three without thinking this unusual. There are no formal organizations with entrance rites (except monasteries) to mark affiliation with one of these traditions to the exclusion of the others. They are more like schools of thought or movements than specific social groups.

Confucianism then is to a great extent an outsider's invention. A Chinese person is more likely to think that Confucius is the leading teacher and formulator of the most ancient tradition of the Chinese culture, and following him is simply part of being Chinese. Chinese people also know of the book ascribed to Lao tzu, the Tao te Ching, as well as various teachings and texts derived from or about the Indian teacher called the Buddha. That these are all axial period shifts from previous cultural and religious traditions is neither generally known by nor important for the Chinese as believers. The Chinese have the choice to draw from any of these resources and more in living and reflecting on life without declaring the kind of affiliation we would expect. Nevertheless, it is not meaningless for us to use "-ism" language and regularize, as the Chinese have not, the variety of religious and philosophical sources on which they draw, as long as we realize that we are distorting the reality by so abstracting and formalizing it. There are ways of speaking clearly even about unclear situations.

There are many more religions and many more names. This summary provides a sketch of the issues involved in such naming while also reviewing the most prominent examples. I hope that the reader of this chapter will never again be tempted to assume that religions are simple things or that their various names are equally legitimate. The situation is subtler and more interesting than that.

5 | NON-RELIGION

It is to be expected that if defining religion (and the religions) is difficult, defining the absence of it (them) also has its problems. If we are to combat prejudice through awareness, we must be self-conscious about the presuppositions involved in non-religious and anti-religious terms. The absolutely impartial, disinterested stance is an impossible ideal despite our efforts in that direction, and thus we must be alert to ulterior purposes and meanings of all sorts, both religious and non-religious.

"Modern" may or may not have implications of being non-religious but it is an important word in the study of religion and deserves some attention before we proceed to more obvious words for non-religion. The oldest and simplest meaning of modern is the present age. Questions arise as to when this age began, what are its characteristics, and, curiously, when it may have ended. The last factor first: some people say that modern has been used so much in the past to refer to the then-present, that insofar as we are now in a new period of time with new defining features we live in a post-modern age. Post-modernity names a widespread suspicion that the misgivings about our objectivity mentioned above, are very justifiable. It can be argued, however, that such suspicion and re-examination of our knowledge is itself a part of the modern mentality, which is highlighted by the post-modernist program.

As to the beginning of the modern, there are those who say that the last major change in religious history was the axial period;

therefore modem religions and the modern age began around 500 BCE. Modernity in this very broad sense consists of the elements introduced by the axial period, the shift from nature to culture, the emphasis on human society and the destiny of the individual human being, and a new reflective self-consciousness.

Modern, however, is usually associated with much later changes and ages. Common is the usage which finds the modern in the technological, social, and intellectual developments in Europe since the sixteenth century Renaissance and Reformation, with anticipations in earlier centuries. In this sense, modern refers to a set of elements which occurred first in Europe, giving the Western world an edge in power during the last four centuries and which only now is becoming dominant in the non-Western world. The elements of the modern world in this sense are an inter-related group of factors, no one of which can exist fully without the others. The most obvious of these factors are technological and economic, i.e., the development of mass production and distribution of manufactured goods. Modern industry and technology, however, are not created or developed in every cultural situation; they must be based in a certain intellectual climate, one which prizes experiment, change, and discovery instead of placing greater weight on stability and authority. Traditions are questioned, revised or abandoned in the light of experiment and rational analysis. In the social realm modernity is expressed in urbanization, the specialization of labor, and the gradual replacement of landed aristocracies by a mercantile middle class. Means of communication and transportation produce pluralistic societies or at least awareness of other worldviews. Individuals pursue their own careers and associations, have geographical and social mobility, and compete with or join others as a matter of personal decision.

These and many other factors characterize the modern as it has been defined in the West to refer to the West. There is a lively debate among peoples who have not been modern in most senses until recently as to whether it is possible to be modern in a way that is very different from the West. All the rest of the world is labeled "traditional" by contrast with the modern, even though those traditions can be quite different from each other. They do share, however, an orientation to the past and resistance to change, in contrast to the hallmarks of modernity. Certainly these traditional characteristics are also found to some extent in modern societies but they do not set the tone and are themselves different within the modern context. What is traditional in traditional societies may be named reactionary in a modern context. It will at least be considered conservative.

Modernity is an example of non-religion to the extent that religion is sometimes understood to be a part of the traditional, pre-modern, world but out of place and waning in the modern world. There are many ways in which the relationship between religion and modernity can be conceptualized, dependent in turn on the definition of each term. At one end of the spectrum there are those for whom religion is replaced by the elements of modernity. If, for example, religion is associated with authority and the preservation of static laws and ideas revealed long ago, then the modern characteristics of intellectual search, questioning, innovation, and progress seem to be inevitably antagonistic to religion. In this kind of analysis, one must be either modern or religious; both at the same time would demand severe compromise or schizophrenia.

There are those, however, who would in various ways update traditional religions to make them more modern. This approach would say that the religions are and should be as capable of re-examination, change, and development as any other area of human life. In this view, there is no conflict between modernity and being religious. A modern religion might have to abandon some of its ancient characteristics, however, in order to preserve the essentials in new forms.

Third, one may argue that religions are essentially concerned with the spirit or some otherwise named arena of human life that remains the same no matter how radically the context of living changes. This argues that religions never were really about those matters which conflict with modern science. Instead, religion is about human things which defy modern mentality or technology. These are things like the meaning and purpose of human life, the solution to feelings of failure and frustration, and the hope for peace between people and within.

These three positions on the relationship of religion and modernity permeate our thoughts and language concerning religion today. They are to be seen within the religious groups, as theologians try to understand and relate their religious heritages to the threats and opportunities of the modern situation. They also are matters of concern in the academic world which attempts to understand this process of reacting to modernity within religious groups.

A word often associated with modern is "secular." Again there is ambiguity concerning the extent and nature of the non-or anti-religious meanings of this word. Secular has an interesting history in which the religious connotation has gone from one extreme to the other. The Latin *saeculum* seems to have started as the word for a generation, the average age of a person's life. From that basis it came to mean a period of time, the age or era, which might last much longer than any one person would live. Christianity has had a doctrine of "ages" wherein the Hebrew-Jewish experience prior to Jesus was the old age, the Christian era the present age, and a millennium and/or eschaton (end of the world) in the future. *Saeculum* was used in Western Christianity as a term for these ages. A liturgical phrase translated into English by "world without end" or "forever and ever" is in Latin *in saecula saeculorum*, i.e., "to the ages of the ages."

In Medieval Latin usage, however, *saeculum* became associated with the present age more than with the others, and thus with the world as it is, compared to what it might yet be. From this kind of reasoning, secular came to be used for things of the world as distinct from things more associated with the next or higher world of being. So a priest was called secular if he served in the world, instead of being a monk, i.e., a "regular" (under a rule) or "religious" (fully devoted to religious activities) priest. In the Middle Ages *saeculum* is definitely a religious term, but it begins to serve as a term for the non-religious. It is used for those aspects of the world and this age which are not under ecclesiastical jurisdiction, such as civil courts and education in subjects other than theology.

It is important to note that this usage implies no antagonism to things religious, only a distinction or separation. Things are called secular in this use of the word when they have no specifically religious character. Only a theology in which believers think that every aspect of personal, social, and intellectual life must be explicitly religious could take exception to the notion that there are secular or non-religious matters in ordinary individual and communal life. It is, however, a matter of degree among religions and religious people just how much of human thought and action is considered to be religiously irrelevant and how much a matter of religious determination. There are, for example, religious groups for whom some food and eating procedures are religiously significant, while for others eating is religiously neutral, that is secular.

Modernity as defined above includes the expansion of the public non-religious arena in which many significant aspects of human life are considered to be religiously irrelevant. Secularization basically refers to the process of change from the specifically religious to the non-religious in various areas of human activity. Before the modern mentality prevails, government, for example, is intimately associated with religious authority if not identical with it. This was true in the pre-axial period civilizations but also to some extent in the later religions, despite their international spread. Since the French and American revolutions, however, more and more political constitutions have dissociated civil government from religious institutions.

The aura of religiosity lingers in the practices of many modern nations. Some have called this phenomenon "civil religion." It demonstrates the persistence of religion in some areas of life despite the conscious intention to remove it. In these two revolutions we see the two possibilities for living and understanding secularization. The French revolution was self-consciously opposed to religion, but the American contained religious as well as non-religious dimensions.

For many people, however, secularization seems like a retreat for the religions. If religion is explicitly involved with fewer activities in human life, this indicates for them a growing weakness, and forebodes an eventual eclipse of religion as a part of human life. In this usage, whether the speaker is pro or con, secularization means the abandonment or destruction of religion. Hence secular comes to mean the anti-religious, no longer neutral to but deleterious to religion. It all depends, of course, on what one takes to be the essential role and provenance of a specific religion or religion in general. If one conceives of a religion as essentially and inevitably involved in government, social regulation, all kinds of educational subjects, etc., then the secular tone that dominates modern life is deplorable. However, people who define religion primarily with reference to its private, experiential aspects, or to its concern with questions concerning the meaning or purpose of human life, are much less likely to understand secularization as a threat to religions. In fact, some religious people welcome secularization as a kind of cleansing of religious institutions from what, in their perspective, are irrelevant concerns.

The most extreme definition of secular is one that goes beyond any concern with religion at all. The most secular person is one for whom religion and the religions have no meaning whatsoever. There are those who apparently are indifferent to the whole list of things associated with religion. If no area of life, personal or public, has an ultimate meaning, any mystical depth, or any transcendent value, indeed the whole of life is secular. There is some question as to how many people there are like that in the world. People who are sympathetic to the role of religion in human life are always on the look-out for hints or rumors of things religious in even the most consistently secular people. Albert Camus was one of the most persistent portrayers and examiners of life lived without reference to anything in the least religious, but there are those who see this position slipping in his last novel, *The Fall.* Most people, I suspect, lead lives that are quite ambiguous on this point. Some of their lives and thoughts are explicitly religious, some implicitly religious, and much else secular by most definitions.

There are many other words and categories for the non-or anti-religious; some of them are not necessarily connected with the modern world and its secularization. One can make a word indicating opposition to anything just by putting "anti-" in front of the name. This is common and not very remarkable as a language phenomenon in most instances. One example of this formation is unusual, however, both for its prevalence and its ambiguity. "Semitic" referred originally to numerous languages of the Near East, including Arabic and Hebrew. In Germany around the end of the nineteenth century, however, a racist organization was formed which was opposed to Jews (and to Christianity too because of its Jewish background). This group used the term "anti-Semitic" to describe its position, perhaps in an attempt to make it sound more scholarly than "anti-Jewish" or "anti-Judaism."

In addition to words of opposition to specific groups, many peoples and languages have words that mean in effect everybody except us. The Greeks thought that other languages sounded like "bar-bar-bar" and called other nations *barbaroi,* whence the English word "barbarians." The Hebrew and Greek words for non-Jews, as used by Jews, are *goyim* and *ethnoi* which are translated as "gentiles" or sometimes "heathen" in English Bibles. Gentile is relatively neutral but heathen, and also pagan have been used often with a tone of contempt. The latter two words are both derived from words meaning the countryside and they reflect the fact that Christianity thrived first in cities, while pre-Christian beliefs and practices persisted among the nature-oriented farmers.

"Infidel" has been used by Christians and Muslims to name the people outside their religious group, the ones who do not have faith (*fides* in Latin). These words, based on religious judgments and ethnocentric perspectives, probably should not be used in the objective study of religion, because they always retain some feeling of negative prejudice. They do, however, tell us something about the ethnocentrism of most peoples and religions, a fact which any study of religion must take into account.

"Heresy" is a term that also reflects a judgmental stance, but in a different way. The heretic, unlike the pagan, has been at some time considered a part of the religion from which viewpoint the word is used. Heresy is not non-religion nor simple anti-religion, but departure from, and rejection of, the proper religion. The root word in Greek means choice or preference, and seems thus to indicate that a kind of willful mistake is involved. A survey of positions and movements called heresies in Christian history gives credence to the theory that heretics are isolated and labeled by the dominant group precisely when they decide to take a stand on some specific issue, argue it without compromise, and choose holding it over submitting to the prevailing powers. Most religious movements spawn new movements and ideas. If the new replaces the old or at least becomes the stronger sentiment, the old is forgotten or suppressed. But if the new is too obviously a departure from the old or is too weak to carry the day, it will be called heretical or whatever comparable word another language provides. Another word for departure from a religion is "apostasy." Usage of this term emphasizes the abandonment of a belief system without any implication of the adoption of an alternative system.

Two words which are associated with the non-or anti-religious are "agnostic" and "atheist." In some circles they are used interchangeably and mean one who rejects all religion. These words can be used more carefully, however, and interesting distinctions can thus be revealed. The "a-" in both words is a privative prefix meaning not something. These terms therefore literally mean "not a knower" and "not a believer in God" (more on "theism" and its compounds in a later chapter on language for beliefs in god or gods).

"Agnostic" was coined in 1869 by Thomas Huxley who chose to use it instead of atheist for his own position, namely that religious matters are unprovable. In its literal sense, it can also be used by believers who distinguish between faith and knowledge. Such religious persons are technically agnostic in affirming that they do not know but rather believe the tenets of their religions, even though other believers make more serious knowledge claims. Atheism is the stronger word in that it definitely rejects any doctrine of God, known or believed. An interesting twist is observable here. Since some religions are not concerned with doctrines of God or gods, the clearest example being Theravada Buddhism, it is possible to be atheistic and religious at the same time. Thus we see that both agnostic and atheist can apply either to people who are self-consciously not religious or to religious people who hold certain attitudes and beliefs.

Returning to the issue of modernism and secularity, the question may be asked: If religion and the religions have been left behind in the process of modernization, what, if anything, has taken their place? Or, working from a different theoretical base: Are there aspects of the modern world which might be appropriately called religious even though they are not usually put in that category? Are there substitutes for religion, or crypto-religions, in the modern world? There are words which reflect these questions and indicate a response to them to which we should give some attention.

What are we to make, for instance, of the word "ideology"? Literally, ideology merely means knowledge of ideas. It has been used to refer to a branch of philosophy, the science of ideas, and to a specific philosophical position, that ideas are derived from sense experience. These uses are not as much of interest to the study of religion as is another application of the word, that is, to a system of beliefs. Not just any system of beliefs but one which the speaker considers to be incorrectly understood or improperly grounded is called an ideology. There is a sense in the word that resembles the use of myth (to be considered in a later chapter) in that both words often refer to the beliefs of others which the user of the word does not share. Ideology has also been used for those sets of beliefs which are promoted for underlying unstated reasons. In this sense, ideology is close to propaganda, as a deliberate program to spread a set of conceptions with ulterior purposes in mind. An ideology can, therefore, be a substitute for religion as a set of beliefs, and ideology can also be a false religion, as a superficial, obfuscating display of ideas.

Even more interesting in this context is the use of "humanism." Literally, the word is not very specific, for all it denotes is a system of thought concerning human beings. It has come to be used, however, for an affirmation of human potentiality and significance that can be thought to be traditionally religious, anti-religious, or a substitute religiosity. Humanism has specifically been associated in the history of Western thought with the Renaissance return to the Greeks and the spirit of ancient philosophy, as compared to the Medieval emphasis on the authorities of church and revelation. Here humanism is a matter of method and spirit, emphasizing individual inquiry plus the limitations and prospects of the human condition. For many people in the Western intellectual tradition this kind of humanism was not and is not essentially anti-religious, even though it does indicate a certain attitude and focus for thought which not all religious groups or traditions share. There are those, therefore, who have called themselves "Christian humanists" and "Jewish humanists," with no sense of this being a contradiction in terms.

There are others, however, for whom humanism is a deliberate alternative to theism. Instead of basing thought and action on revelation or any notion of God or gods, this humanism builds an approach to the understanding and direction of life on reasonable inquiry and confidence in the human enterprise. There is much that can be said in support of this kind of humanism as a religion or substitute for religion. Certainly Buddhism and Confucianism can be understood to be humanistic in this sense, and humanistic thought in Western societies often provides a sense of meaning to human life comparable to that found in the traditional religions.

There is also a third use of humanism, coupled with secular, that means for its users something that is opposed to religion in every way. From this point of view, humanism is atheistic and human-centered in a way that is deliberately antagonistic to religious concerns and principles. Perhaps it is a sign of the distress many religious people feel at the phenomenon of secularization that secular humanism should have such bad connotations for them. Meanwhile, other religious people for whom the secular character of public affairs in modern societies is desirable find both words, secular and humanism, inoffensive or religiously positive.

Another word on which there are almost diametrically opposed meanings and associations is "materialism." It is a commonplace of religious preaching to condemn concern for wealth and physical property as materialistic. The expressed or implied notion is that the materialist has a foolish or sinful dependency on possessing things, most or all of which are dangerous or harmful. By contrast, materialism as a philosophical position affirms the reality of the physical world. In this sense it may be used to describe Western theologies as compared with Gnostic ideas and the doctrine of maya in Hinduism. The latter doctrines say that the material world is ultimately illusory. So when the Western religions emphasize the creation of a good world by a good God they are materialistic in this second sense. A third meaning, also philosophical, is based on the premise that matter is all there is and that the mind and its creations are all understandable in terms of brain processes. The first and third definitions of materialism are non-or anti-religious but the second is religious.

As we so often have to conclude: the changing definitions and conceptions of religion change the use and character of words about religion. If some sort of transcendent, holy, super-empirical reality is essential to any proper use of religion, then most of the words we have been examining do indeed fall into the non-religion category. But if one takes the approach that religion can be defined without this particular element, then the borderline becomes unclear. It may be possible to say many interesting and valuable things by seeing modernity, humanism, and much else as religious in some sense, in some ways.

6 | THE STUDY OF RELIGIONS

Adjectives are often ambiguous. What do you think might be meant by the words "religious scholarship"? It could mean scholarship or study performed in a religious way by religious people. But it is possible to understand it to mean scholarship about religion performed by anyone, religious or not. There are university departments which are called departments of religious studies, but they are located in secular institutions with no idea of practicing religion. (They are religious only in that very broad sense of the term in which devotion and intense interest are called religious metaphorically.)

The distinction is important enough to fuss over, since universities, and especially those funded by public funds, have no business being religious, that is, affirming specific doctrines and practices. In addition to these, however, there are academic institutions which deliberately think, teach, and work within a theological framework. This means that they clearly affirm certain religious affiliation and conviction. Secular universities which do not have religious affiliation, nevertheless, should provide classes and other forums for the analysis of the religious activities and thoughts of people near and far, because religion is so much a part of human life.

Not all our words for the study of religion are clearly in either the theological or secular camps. The difference between these kinds of study is often identifiable only after close examination of a speaker's or author's presuppositions and conclusions.

Religious and ideological commitment can hide beneath apparently objective analysis, especially in the apologetic mode of theological discourse.

We can illustrate this issue by returning to the problem of naming university departments and fields of study. To avoid the ambiguity of "religious studies" some alternatives have been adopted. "Comparative religions" was used years ago but has been largely abandoned because it concentrated attention on only one of the methods or activities of the study of religions, the comparison of correlative phenomena. "History of religions" is used at the University of Chicago and is perhaps too narrowly identified with that school. Also the history in that name is not restricted to events of the past although that is the most common meaning of the word history. "Religion studies" might do the job, but even better are the word combinations which specify the plural, religions, because pluralism is the most telling characteristic of objective study. Frederick Max Muller said, "To know one is to know none." Thus one cannot study religion unless one knows a number of religions. Knowing only one religion almost guarantees the confusion of the specific with the generic and presumptions of normativity.

One way of rejecting this principle has been adopted by some Christians who say, "Christianity begins where religion ends," thus excluding their religion from the general study of religions. Other religious people similarly can be put off by the notion that outsiders or an objective, descriptive approach can do any justice to their deeply held beliefs and practices. People do not like to have their religions examined by uncommitted observers. Despite this fear of invasion or misinterpretation, it is inevitable that religious speech, texts, and behavior become to some extent public and then it is subject to comment, no matter how just or unfair. Like it or not, if a religious tradition gets to be important and powerful, people will talk about it and form theories about it. Christianity displays many thoughts and practices comparable to those of other religions. It looks like a religion even if some of its elements might be unusual or unique. Excluding it from the category of religion is illegitimate, even if it has certain theological or insiders' justification.

Another suggestion for naming the field of study concerned with religions is "phenomenology." In philosophy this is a movement associated with Edmund Husserl in the beginning of the twentieth century. It is a middle position between idealism and realism in that it concentrates on the interaction of subject and object without rejecting the role of either in human knowledge. When this position is applied to the study of religion, it emphasizes the creative role of the investigator and scholar in the understanding which is achieved. It does not, however, reject such knowledge as pure fabrication or fiction. Without necessarily examining the epistemological details of this position, students of religions apply it to their analysis of religious thought and behavior. They understand the product of their research in a phenomenological way if and when they see it as an interpretive construction which enables them to understand what appears to them as religious. Even if it does not prescribe a method, this philosophical position provides a tone or attitude for the scholar, one of modesty and respectful attention.

What religious people may fear in the secular study of religion is commonly called "reductionism." This is criticized by objective students of religion too. Reductionism results, in part, from the division of scholarly labor on religion. If each field of study takes its peculiar aspect of religion to be the basic or definitive one, it will tend to reduce all that is religious to functions or effects of its chosen focus. Watch out for the statements that begin: "Religion is nothing but . . ." or "Religion is just . . . ." It is tempting, of course, to feel that one has found the golden key to so powerful and complex a phenomenon as religion, and the sense of control in a new methodology is especially attractive. Thus some people have been inclined to see all religion in terms of psychological dynamics or social needs, to give two prominent examples. People concerned with understanding religion should be wary of simplistic analyses.

Closely related to reductionism and other problems in the study of religions is the word "science" and its various meanings. German scholars have named the religion-studies discipline *Religonswissenschaft*, i.e., the science of religions. If science is defined in reference to its usual subject matter, the juxtaposition of religion and science seems strange, because that usual subject matter is the physical world. Certainly some religious phenomena are accessible to the kind of measurement and verification used in the sciences. Here we could include experiments on the brain activities of people engaged in religious meditation, carbon dating of religious artifacts, and similar investigations. These matters are peripheral to most religiosity.

However, if the sciences are defined by their common methodology, new possibilities appear. When we extend science to include the social sciences, much more relevant material is available. People can study scientifically, although without the rigor of the laboratory, many psycho-social and historical religious phenomena. As science these investigations are marked by care in theoretical construction, attention to empirical data, and verification procedures.

Science, historically, is closely related to the words for knowledge and varies with one's analysis of what constitutes knowledge. Aristotle defined science as certain knowledge based on necessary principles. Taking certain and necessary in their strictest senses that definition narrows science to very little of what we want to know about our world. Most of our knowledge would seem to be calculated guess-work. No matter how uncertain the rest of human knowledge is, it seems clear to most scholars that the arena of religious speculation or revelation is the least certain. We are not speaking here of the unscientific nature of religious doctrine, having assumed from the beginning that gods, heavens, and souls are matters of faith and belief. It is the very knowledge of human religious activity that is elusive enough to be pretty much inaccessible to scientific method.

Therefore, there is a range of meanings for the applicability of science to religion that runs from the optimistic to the pessimistic. Some people will feel that much significant knowledge can be gained by applying scientific methods to religious matters. Others will call their assumptions or convictions about human religiosity science or knowledge, whether they have been subject to scientific method or not. Yet others, however, will be convinced that so much understanding of religions is tentative and speculative that they will be loath to use the word science for it at all. One may hope, nevertheless, that the pessimists will not abandon all care and responsibility in their study of religion. Even if little can be known and scientific precision is unattainable, students of religion can talk meaningfully about the probabilities and work towards clarity in the details, so that a modest confidence about knowing religion can be achieved.

Relevant to much of this discussion is the notion of a worldview. The religions themselves, other ideologies, and the various scientific or academic fields of study can all be seen as views or perspectives on the world. Taken most radically this implies that we all make our own worlds, seeing, analyzing, and talking about only what we have constructed in our minds. Even if this radical position is modified by some idea of input from the external world, it is fairly obvious that each person develops a set of mental pictures which can be quite wrong on occasion, as optical illusions and paranoia illustrate. Often we get along in the world, even with somewhat erroneous or skewed views of reality, especially if our view is derived from prevailing views in our society. Every social group shares a common set of presuppositions and expectations, and socializes its young by inculcating these shared notions. Worldviews can be used as a more inclusive term than religions, but in much the same way, to name the individual, or more often, the shared interpretations of reality. A worldview is the set of beliefs and symbols, deep in human consciousness, which gives cultures a sense of identity and makes them identifiable to observers.

Examinations of thought systems, from scientific to religious, recently has emphasized the process of theoretical construction. It has been noted that scientific schools and religious traditions in somewhat similar ways build models of reality based on basic assumptions or axioms which are themselves speculative or unverifiable. Human thought elaborates and applies such systems, and persists in doing so even when undesirable or contradictory results ensue, until the inadequacy of the system and its assumptions are so clear that a brand new start must be made. In scientific endeavors the repudiation of old theories and the development of new might be more necessary and frequent, but other arenas of analysis ultimately follow the same pattern. Religions of the past have been superseded by new responses to the religious needs of people, sometimes because these needs have changed. New insights or revelations become the basis for a new theological construction by which to understand the world and live successfully. As this process is apparent in the sciences and in religions, it is also to be observed in the social sciences and the study of religion. Theories regarding the basic nature of religiosity come and go based on various assumptions concerning the root of the phenomenon and its dynamics. In the study of religion, one must be aware, therefore, of the processes of theory construction and theory change in both the observed and the observer, the human objects of study and the human subject studying them.

The words "model" and "paradigm" are used frequently in this kind of discussion. The latter is used in grammatical studies where the inflections or changes of form in one word are taken as an example for all the rest in that group. Thus it is a dominant example in the teaching and study of its category, and can be distinguished from a model which is not a member of the group but another kind of thing which has reference to some thing or group of things. The model is an abstraction and a fiction which is

constructed to represent the essential nature or activity of something. A few examples might help here. A Christian theological
theory of the atonement like the ransom theory (Jesus pays the
ransom to the devil for human beings) is a model but the behavior of Jesus is a paradigm for proper human life. Pre-animism is
a model for how religions make sense to primitive peoples; the
Melanesian concept of *mana* is the paradigm by which scholars
understood other words and beliefs all over the world.

Other words used in and of the various sciences or by
philosophers are used also in the study of religions. The words in
this paragraph certainly are not unique to investigations of religion
but they are problematic in any context. "Empirical," for example,
seems straight-forward enough; it refers to the evidence of the
senses. Reflection on the experience of the senses and the
interpretation of it, however, has brought many people to the
conviction that there is no uninterpreted experience, all data is
theory-laden. Strict empiricism would seem to be, therefore,
impossible. The words, rational and rationalism are even more
vexed. They start out with apparently clear reference to the orderly
thinking functions of the mind, to reason as comprehension,
understanding, and explanation. Further reflection, as usual,
discloses problems in this notion. Primarily, we note a continuum
of meanings from trustworthy reason to deliberately duplicity as
rationalization, the veneer of rationality. In that continuum we
become aware that what is rational to one may be absurd to
another, what is reasonable to one is incredible to another.

The philosophical study of religion focuses on issues like
the rationality of religious statements, sometimes with reference
to supposed empirical evidence but also in purely abstract terms.
So-called "proofs" for the existence of God are prominent in this
realm of discourse. They are taken to be cogent by some people
who, therefore, see denial of God's existence as stupidity and
foolishness. Others see faults and holes in their arguments and
thus legitimate the rationality of agnosticism or atheism. Another
line of investigation avoids the question of existence and focuses

on the nature of belief and the sense of rationality or reasonableness that people have regarding religious conceptions. In this context the scholar asks what conviction is and what convinces some people while leaving others skeptical. These issues can be investigated as psycho-social matters as much as intellectual, and they underline the role of society in the construction of reality.

Part of the difference here can be understood by noting the philosophers' distinction between "true" and "valid." Validity addresses the correctness of an argument, its internal consistency from premises to inferences and conclusions. Truth deals with statements and the facts of the world to which such statements are deemed to be adequate. Religious arguments, therefore, may be valid but false, or true but invalid.

"History" has come up in many contexts in the study of religions. It is a problem word and a problem concept or set of concepts. Let us begin, as we often do, with an attempt to define the most common perception of the word and then review the other meanings as refinements or departures from that basis. At the broadest level people take history to mean the total events of the past, as they actually were. One immediate refinement limits this to the human past and excludes natural history. A further refinement limits history to the recorded past and therefore calls earlier human activity "prehistoric." Recognition of the role of recording history shifts attention from the events of the past to the words about those events and history is seen to be oral or written accounts of what happened. At this point we realize that the speakers and writers of histories select from the many events that are known to them and also portray them in selected ways. Thus a history is understood to be based on a particular selection of what is historic, and to be a particular interpretation. There can be quite different accounts of the same events or other histories of the same times, focused on different events.

When the interpretive character of history-telling is fully examined, one can become quite skeptical about the possibility of knowing history as past events at all. It seems we are left only with people's distorted views. It may be that the more histories we have the more we may be able to filter out the individual bias, but a pervasive bias may elude even this test. Thus, history as a version of the selected past merges into myth, as will be discussed in chapter 8 on religious language. The main point of the conjunction there and here is to recognize the role the story plays in human life and not necessarily to comment on its factuality. A sacred history, despite its similarity to other historical accounts, becomes sacred when a group of people take the presumed events and the written account of them to be determinative in understanding self, society, the world, and the future.

A hallmark of sacred history is its pre-occupation with its meaning for subsequent peoples. This tends to include descriptions which modern people see as non-factual elaboration on what really happened. For example, miraculous birth stories of Moses, the Buddha, and Jesus are widely thought to be more creative than reportorial, by people both within and outside the circles of faith. Such extravagant elements in the histories underline the religious function of the accounts. Sacred histories are not casual or disinterested records but enthusiastic proclamations of the crucial events of all time. The events themselves are, ultimately, less important than their meaning and may even be adjusted so that the meaning is clearer.

Another characteristic of histories, especially those with religious significance, is the shape or direction of the accounts. Almost all historical writing, except the most bland chronicle, presumes some movement, and maybe even purpose, behind or within events. The first contrast we notice is that between cyclical and linear histories, those that end up where they began and those that can never go back. Some people say that cyclical history is not really history, and of course it is not in the Western, linear conception of the term. Whether we call them histories or not, some conceptions of time seem to be based on, or parallel in structure to, the course of the natural seasons. In this pattern every

Spring is a return to Spring, and the history of the year has come full circle to its beginning again. The cycle can be yearly or based on some larger unit, perhaps called an age, eon, era, *yuga* (in Hinduism), or *saeculum* (see the discussion of "secular" in chapter 5). Linear history sees every Spring as a new Spring and every event as unrepeatable. Events of the past can change the rest of history. Time has high points, special moments, sometimes categorized by a form of the Greek *kairos*, such as "kairotic," to contrast with *chronos*, the kind of time measured by a clock with each moment the same as any other. For the religious traditions of the West since the axial era and Zoroaster, time and history have also had an end, or *eschaton*, but secular linear histories may not share that expectation.

A second contrast is between a downward and upward slant to the historical line. Cycles can, of course, spiral downward as they do in the Hindu pattern of *yugas*, leading to the periodic dissolution of the world and its subsequent re-creation. It is clearer with linear views that the line might be flat, jagged, or over-all progressive or regressive. Western religious eschatology has been basically regressive. The world as the battle between good and evil forces becomes ever more violent until the final battle destroys the world as we know it. This is the major pattern in Jewish and Christian apocalyptic mythology and literature, to be discussed more later. Since the Renaissance period in Western history, however, a progressive, evolutionary pattern for understanding history has become more popular. In spite of occasional times of decline, the general course of history is seen to be a matter of increasing complexity, capability, and success. Whether it is explicitly religious or not, such an optimistic view of the course of the world into the future is as mythological as the sacred histories which interpret the past.

The suffix "-ism" added to many words just indicates a category name, as in the naming of religions reviewed in chapters 3 and 4. The same suffix, however, can add a tone of religion-like commitment and intolerance in other combinations. Some-ism words are invented in order to identify and criticize the supposed assumptions of other people. Thus we find historicism used to name a position which takes all periods of time to be relative in meaning and accomplishment to all others, beyond which there are no absolute truths or references. Relativism similarly identifies the suspicion of absolute truth-claims whether their historical grounding is mentioned or not. Pluralism is a related word which emphasizes the many claims to a correct understanding of the world and life which are apparent in the modern scene. It is especially relevant to the study of contemporary religion because previously isolated traditions now confront each other. In some instances pluralism is deplored and in other cases leads to friendly conversation. Ecumenism is sometimes used to name such positive contacts or it can refer to attempts, chiefly within Christianity, to unite previously separate religious groups into one organization.

A relatively new-ism which affects the study of religion is "feminism." This word can refer to the claim that women and men should not be distinguished in many of the arenas of human life in which such distinctions previously have been made: law, politics, economics, society. If distinctions are to be made in these areas, the basic feminist position maintains, they should cross gender lines, e.g. in the search for the best person to fill a political office. Feminism in the academic world has also meant directing scholarly attention to the activity of women in studies of human thought and behavior. These studies often go beyond the events and texts in which male participation dominates to those arenas of human life where women work, e.g. shifting from military to social history. In that semi-religious character of "ism", feminism names a movement which promotes changes in thought and society with marked fervor and commitment. In compensation for the predominance of male dominance in history and the writing of history, a feminist position may argue for the dominance of women, in the past, now, or in the future. The theory of a matriarchal period in human prehistory has been argued in this context

Certainly there are many-isms to name schools of thought. One could go on at great length mentioning and characterizing them. Arbitrarily I shall select only one more, because it is prominent, confusing, and perhaps typical. My choice is "structuralism" which is associated especially with Claude Levi-Strauss. The essence of this approach to religious materials is the shift of attention from individual items in a system to their inter-relationships. The events, symbols, and characters of a myth, for example, should not be isolated from context in the story, but understood as parts of a pattern, usually a set of polarities, within the story and thus also the worldview of the society in which the myth is created and told. We are not to think of Oedipus as simply a tragic hero but as one reference in a web of dichotomies which manifest in narrative the Greek notion of nature versus culture. Like many other movements in scholarly or intellectual circles, structuralism is presented at first as the only or best way of studying the material. Later scholarship tends to incorporate its insights within a larger collection of methods and results, or increasingly ignores it.

7 | RELIGIOUS EXPERIENCE

A number of words have been used in an attempt to name and describe religious experience, the psychological or interior component of religions. As was mentioned in the second chapter, the definitions which locate the essence of religion in private experiences of awe and worship have been popular in the study of religion. Joachim Wach, for example, understood all the public forms and materials of religions to be expressions of the basic, formative experiences of founders and believers. This gives the experiential component a priority in the development of anything that might be called religious. To be fair to other theories and possibilities, however, it should be noted that in the actual lives of peoples and cultures the other features of religion may be more basic, essential, and prior. The rites, morals, texts, and social institutions might come first, without any intense or even modest experiential component, that is without some previous private mystical experience. In other words, it might be a theoretical, cultural, or religious prejudice to assume that special states of consciousness produce public religious phenomena rather than the other way around. In any event, this chapter is given over to those words which attempt to designate the ways in which people feel religiously.

Rudolf Otto popularized the word "numinous" to serve as a term for the core religious experience upon which he thought all religion was ultimately based. The term is derived from one of the Latin words for the sacred, but is developed by Otto to be a special word in his theory of religious emotion. That which is numinous for a human being, according to Otto, is that which elicits strong feelings of attraction and fear at the same time. From one experience to another, terror or beneficence might predominate, but both are constitutive elements in the crucial, basic experience of the holy, wholly other, presence.

Words associated with numinous are awe, tremendous (in its root sense of something which inspires trembling), power or "majesty (recognition of power before which one is weak and dependent), mystery, fascination, magic, and miracle. In his analysis Otto stresses the contradictory feelings which signal the experience of holiness; it is the emotional correlate of paradox in theology. Its contradictory character and psychic power are demonstrations of the non-rational and non-ethical essence of the numinous. Although there are obviously ideas and values that flow from the experience, the experience is different from thought or will, and is the irreducible heart of all the rest of religion.

There are other ways of describing or naming the kind or kinds of experience that are important in religious life. Abraham Maslow has used the term "peak experience" to refer to a state of consciousness in which someone feels unusually joyful, creative, lucky, unbounded. This experience is not necessarily religious for the experiencer or the observer, but this non-religious description of a special experience might help outsiders to understand what some religious people say about their special moments.

In religious contexts this whole area of extraordinary states of mind or states of consciousness has been associated with the word "mysticism." This is a much-used word which requires a lot of attention. At the most casual level its superficial similarity to "misty" seems to play a part, for people use it to refer to anything in religion which is hazy or unclear. The related word mystery also plays a part, the common notion of something mysterious being that which is not clearly known. Both mysticism and mystery are derived from ancient Greek words used of secret cults and their initiates, for example the mystery cult headquartered at Eleusis and the followers of Dionysos. The essential element of these cults themselves may or may not have been their secrecy or esotericism, but that is what they were famous for. Sociologically, the cults' preservation of secret rites, texts, and symbols was their most distinctive and impressive characteristic. Thus mystery has been used to designate that which is known to be not known; we know there are people who do, say, and read certain things but we do not know what those things are, and are prevented at least temporarily from finding out.

A lot of the meaning of mystery and mysticism, therefore, has to do with the phenomenon of deliberate secrecy. In the case of at least some secret cults or societies the secrets are arbitrary and otherwise knowable. This is the sense in which we call a detective novel a mystery; one does eventually find out what was previously hidden or mysterious, whereupon the mystery is solved and the secret becomes known and public. This kind of secrecy is important in the history of religions and deserves more attention later in connection with the terminology for religious groups. In the present context, however, other kinds of secrecy may be implied by the use of mystery and mysticism.

First, there is something inevitably private, hidden, and thus secret about our experiences as human beings. No one else can see exactly what we see, hear what we hear, let alone feel or think what we individually feel and think. Words like mysticism or religious experience can refer, therefore, to nothing more nor less than the personal, individual, or private dimension of the religious phenomenon. Insofar as one has thoughts and feelings, perceptions and involvement, in and about things in any way religious, one could be said to be participating in the mystical.

Beyond this there is another notion of secrecy or mystery that refers to matters unknown and unknowable even to the self. In addition to being mysteries to others and they to us, we are often mysteries to ourselves. The secrets of the self to the self as well as the secrets of the world and all that is in it are the materials for a deeper mysticism. This mysticism is a recognition of and confrontation with the hidden but suspected things or persons behind things, and ultimately the thing or person behind it all.

Apparently people have different kinds of mystical experiences, or conceive of and describe their own and other people's mystical experiences in a variety of ways. Many types of descriptions have been proposed and people argue for the pre-eminence of one or another of these types, often denigrating the alternatives. For some mystics or theorists of mysticism the overwhelming nature of these experiences of the secret depths of things is emotional or ecstatic. Others stress the calmer, intellectual type of experience, and characteristically associate the emotional experience with some preliminary stages or with people of lesser intelligence or social standing. Just what is considered to be the essential or highest mystical experience must be determined in the case of each writer or tradition. Even though each source will argue for the logic and authority of its assertion there is obviously no way of checking the facts of mystical experiences precisely because they are private and publicly unknowable, both by definition and by the nature of the supposed experience.

In the more emotional understandings of mysticism, the word "ecstasy" is often mentioned. This term can be used in the general sense of intense, exhilarating joy or it might have the literal meaning (given its Greek roots) of being outside of oneself or one's body. The phenomenon of shamanism has been described as the practice of techniques of ecstasy in this literal sense, because the shamans say that they leave their bodies during their dances and trances in order to travel the worlds, retrieve lost spirits, and perform other helpful acts. The literal antonym of "ecstasy" is "enthusiasm" which is derived from words which indicate another way of conceptualizing intense religious emotion, namely possession by a god (*in* plus *theos*, Greek for god). Neither ecstasy nor enthusiasm are used commonly in these special etymological senses. But they do thus illustrate ways in which religious experiences of an extraordinary sort might be understood within various theological talk about special kinds of knowledge or states of awareness which are beyond anything to which words like knowledge in any language are appropriate. Mystical theologies often teach a hierarchy of knowing or consciousness through which one can rise from ignorance to complete enlightenment, union with the mind of the universe, or something comparably ultimate. Words like the Greek term *gnosis* may be used by scholars or the mystics themselves to indicate a transcendent, salvific knowledge. Often such knowledge is described in terms of a unification of knowledge, a state wherein one does not know things separately but whole and at once. All of this eludes normal language which, of course, deals with matters separately and seriatim.

Mystical paths to enlightenment and fulfillment are sometimes described using positive language of growth, attainment, transcendence, etc., but there are also major traditions in which the path and/or the goal are described negatively. In the latter cases emphasis is put on the incapacity of human language and humanity itself to comprehend or even experience the mystic possibility. This attitude produces the pieties of the *via negativa* and the naming of the ultimate goal nirvana, that is "extinction, to give two examples. This attitude also tends to fit better with the notion of an impersonal absolute rather than a personal god, a contrast discussed later under "god language," in Chapter 10.

Some proponents and analysts of mysticism treat it as if it were the essence, source, and end of all religion. It seems to me less prejudicial to see the kinds of practices and ideas associated with mysticism as one type or group of types of religiosity which constitute an option of varying prestige within the religious traditions, sometimes praised and sometimes avoided.

There are other practices, emotions, and thoughts in the religious world than those which are appropriately called "mystic," or are necessarily derivable from this kind of piety. There are, for example, religious situations in which less intense and extraordinary experiences are cultivated and in which more if not most people are expected to have those experiences. The terms "devotionalism" and "pietism" have been used to name styles of religious practice wherein a warming of the heart, deeply felt conversion, feelings of love for the god or goddess, repentance and forgiveness, and the like, are the desired states of being. In this context mention should also be made of the word "charismatic," derived from Christian theology to name the behaviors (and accompanying states of mind and emotion) promoted in some groups. The most important religious experience for many such Christian groups is "speaking in tongues," also named by a transliteration of the word for it in Greek, *glossolalia*. These experiences might be called mystical in some broad usage but are more public and demonstrative than the pursuits and practices of those people usually called "mystics." Nevertheless, they illustrate the larger phenomenon of special and expected forms of consciousness, or even the loss of consciousness, which can be an important part of some religious life.

The twentieth century Jewish philosopher Martin Buber contributed some interesting terminology and analysis in his notion of the "I-Thou." Meeting others as persons rather than as things is for him the essence of distinctively human life. Obviously, the meeting of God as Thou thus constitutes a way of naming and defining religious experience. It is a very modern way of talking about such experience because it does not presume any mythological framework or trans-conscious state of mind, but rather the transference to God of a common daily possibility for human beings. This might be the least flamboyant way of talking about religious experience and the most accessible.

There is a group of words used in the analysis of religions that also deals with extraordinary experiences but with reference to the presumed or supposed cause or object of such experiences. These are the "-phany" words, based on the Greek root *phainein*, to show, and, in the passive, to appear. "Phenomenon" comes from the same root and it means basically an observed event, but especially one that is unusual or one about which one is self-conscious. A whole school of philosophy has resulted from the implications of this word. Much religion study is also called phenomenological because it starts with what actually appears in religious life, compared to what someone thinks should ideally be the case.

The most common of the-phany words is "epiphany" which simply means disclosure or appearance. It is also the name of a Christian holy day, centered on the disclosure to the magi that the child Jesus was a special child, in the Gospel of Matthew. Other-phany words are more specific. "Hierophany" is the appearance of something as holy. "Theophany" is the appearance of a god or goddess. "Kratophany" is the appearance of power. In each case the-phany word indicates a situation in which people describe certain experiences as doorways to the super-normal, as confrontation with a more important reality.

Throughout this chapter it has been difficult to separate matters of the heart from those of the head, emotion from thought, because they do not seem to be clearly different things in human experience. Much of our language, however, does assume such a difference, and in some historical periods much has been made of reason versus feelings or knowledge versus desire. Perhaps this kind of talk indicates poles between which there is a continuum with various mixtures; human consciousness rarely lacks either component at any one time, but we may judge one category or the other to be ascendant. In this chapter, therefore, I have selected words that are associated more with the emotional side of the assumed polarity and in later chapters on doctrines or ideas in religions the intellectual side will be dominant. To be sure, however, there are few if any religious experiences without ideational implications and likewise few doctrines that never arouse intense emotion.

There is a word in English which reflects this state of affairs, namely "faith." On the one hand it is used as a synonym for religious affiliation. In this sense it can be taken to refer to convictions, more or less like a series of intellectual propositions. On the other hand it is used in personal contexts where its synonyms would be trust or confidence, and here the intellectual aspect pales alongside the emotions of personal commitment and love. Much Christian theological writing (especially Protestant) has been concerned with the relative mix of these components. An emphasis on faith as propositional statements is sometimes accused of leaning towards scholasticism or fundamentalism, while an emphasis on the experiential approach is criticized for being too liberal or emotional. As in so many cases, there may be a wisdom in the common, confused usage because it indicates that these poles of human life cannot be separated, and that both mind and heart are involved in faith even though there may be some variation in the mix.

Another way of discussing faith concerns the role of the will. The question is: Does a person decide to have faith? The alternatives to such willing might be supernatural activity or some more subtle mental, emotional, or cultural influences which might produce the state called faith. The approach based on will can be called "voluntarist," and is associated with the writings of Blaise Pascal and William James. On the other side, Martin Luther argues against theological voluntarism in his treatise "On the Bondage of the Will." Behind this discussion lies the problem, especially acute in the Western religions, of the relative powers of human beings and God. If God is all-powerful, then he (or she) decides and determines everything, or at least the most important things, including salvation. But if human beings have some measure of freedom and responsibility, then they decide some things too, perhaps including their salvation. Various positions are espoused from strict predestination to complete free will and autonomy for humanity. This is, of course, a theological dispute and thus often argued in scholarly abstractions, but it is also a matter of great emotional import and concerns the basic religious experience of those involved. At issue is whether one should focus on the feeling of dependence and gratitude towards God, a sense of responsibility for the fate of oneself and the world, or some combination of the two.

There is another area of great theological discussion in Christian circles which also concerns the psychical or experiential side of life: the emotions and ideas referred to by the term "love." It is common in discussions of the word love to note that this English word is very broad and can be subdivided by noting the narrower meanings of three Greek words, *philia*, *eros*, and *agape*. *Philia* is the love between friends, to summarize very briefly. *Eros* is not just sexual love, as its English compounds signify, but all forms of longing for fulfillment and enrichment. By contrast with *eros*, *agape* is a self-giving love which gains little but may lose much because it is a caring and protecting love of another. The controversy here involves one's description of God's love of humanity, a human being's love of God, and a human being's love of other human beings. Some advocate a view of God and the ideal for human beings in terms of *agape* alone and others find room for *eros* too.

Hinduism, especially in the devotion to Krishna, has definitely affirmed an erotic model for piety. In certain Tantric circles and in the old nature religions, sexual activity has had a religious role. In these contexts sexual activity is more important for ritual than emotional reasons, at least according to the descriptions and prescriptions in the texts. By contrast, Krishna devotionalism does not make use of explicit sexual activity in its rituals but uses the phenomenon of human erotic emotion and behavior as an analogy for, and model of, devotion to the god. The Song of Songs in the Hebrew Bible is often read in this light, that is, as an allegory for spiritual love between human beings and God, despite its apparent eroticism. In regard to sexual emotion and activity, as in regard to most other aspects of human life, religions are different in their responses, some affirming and some denying the religious value of sexual or erotic love, either as a symbol or as a part of human life.

Agape love is hardly ever discussed in terms of sexual emotion or activity but may be likened to parental love with an emphasis on the sacrifices involved in providing good for the beloved person. This ideal and an ethics based on it is prominent in Christian thought and is also present in the Buddhist tradition, especially the Mahayana schools. The ideal of the *bodhisattva* who foregoes nirvana in order to assist others in the Buddhist path comes close to the idea of agape in Christianity. The Buddhist *agape* is often designated by the word "compassion" rather than love and this might be a better translation for Christian *agape* too. The Christian terminology is made more complex when charity is used, derived from the Latin *caritas*, the word which Jerome used to translate *agape* in the Vulgate. This is confusing because the common notion of charity is money or other kindnesses given to the needy, and that is at best a special form of *agape* and at worst a dry remnant of it.

All these words that are supposed to refer to interior experience have to be problem words because of the privacy of their object. We must be especially careful in using them and reading them.

8 | RELIGIOUS LANGUAGE

At first glance you might say that this whole book is about religious language, but that would be wrong. It is about language used to describe religions, and that language is not necessarily or essentially religious. Furthermore, this chapter is not among those many investigations into the nature of the language used by religious people (or is so very rarely and incidentally). Instead, it is about the language used in these and other investigations which attempts to name, describe, and analyze the language used by religious people. Is this a little confusing? Perhaps an example will help.

Turning to an example that will figure prominently in this chapter, religious people rarely, if ever, call their own sacred stories "myths," but scholars regularly use that term to designate such sacred stories. Thus, "myth" and the other words under consideration here are of a second order of abstraction; they are words about other words, language about other language.

This chapter tries to explain some of the confusing but important terms which have been used to describe and categorize the verbal aspects of religions, especially oral rather than written words. (Written materials will be the focus of the next chapter.) We will also touch on some things which are not composed of words but which are often discussed in connection with the study of verbal communication, for example religious art. More will be said about art in a later chapter also, in connection with ritual.

Meanwhile, the character of communication and the role of words in it deserve some attention.

The word "language" itself indicates this extended area of investigation. While it refers basically to verbal means of communication, it is also used to refer to other communication systems which are not verbal, for example "body language," "computer language," the language of art, music, and so on. These other means of communication and expression share some of the characteristics of verbal language but not others; nevertheless, verbal language often serves as a model or paradigm for the other languages. Susanne Langer (in *Philosophy in a New Key*) called verbal language, plus close imitators like Morse code, "discursive." The others by contrast were "representational." She emphasized that the latter are not less than, but different, from verbal language in their means of communication and in what they are best in communicating. One must not take the idea of communication here too narrowly; it can include communicating with oneself or merely recording matters without knowing if they will ever be heard or read by anyone else.

Insight into the respective characteristics of verbal and non-verbal systems of communication can be gained through an examination of a number of related terms. "Sign" is a word which is used to denote things with words on them as well as indicators without words. Some scholars appropriate the word "signal" to refer to non-verbal signs. Within the category of sign or signal one can recognize two groups: First there are the signals we read in nature, like thunder as a signal for rain, which might also be called "symptoms," a word used more in connection with medical diagnosis understood as a reading of signs. Second, there are the signals people send to each other in non-verbal ways, including gestures, simple artifacts (e.g., ribbons to mark a woodland trail), and non-verbal noises. Signs and signals usually refer to isolated elements that are not part of a larger system, items that can be understood alone without much if any reference to a pattern or grammar of any sort. Note that many signs or signals are universal among human beings and perhaps also some animals, while verbal languages must be learned.

There is a wider use of sign which includes both signals and the more complex kind of communicative device usually called "symbol." At a very loose and general level of word usage, sign and symbol are synonyms; both refer to anything that is associated with or points to something else and thus conveys some kind of information. Such bland, all-encompassing definitions are not adequate to the subtleties of human communication, however. We need other terms or more restricted definitions of these terms in order to name and discuss different kinds of religious language, as well as other areas of communication. When signal and sign are defined in their narrower senses, symbol is reserved to name a less direct kind of reference device whose primary example and model is verbal language.

A word as a symbol does not just point to or betray the presence of something, it stands for it and replaces it as a device in our thought. If a rattlesnake is about to attack me it might signal its presence with its rattles or another person might gesture or yell to warn me. These are signs or signals. It is quite another thing to take that experience away with me, far from the snake, and transmit it to others without any of the sounds of the incident by using the words "snake," "yell," and "rattle," as in fact I just did. Instead of carrying around the snake to tell my story I can much more conveniently carry around the word, either as sound (the pronunciation of "snake") or the conventions for writing that word or sound. "Snake" symbolizes the animal without being at all like it. Central to this meaning of symbol is the arbitrary, conventional character of the item that stands for something else.

Nothing in all this discussion, however, accounts for another use of symbol, one in which, to use another animal example, the phenomenon of cat, however indicated, serves as a symbol for something other than catness or cats. In other words, the symbol "cat" refers to cats, but cats can symbolize an Egyptian goddess, a witch, bad luck, and many other things and ideas. At this level we are not talking about the mechanisms of simple communication alone but also the ways in which human beings use phenomena (and the names of such phenomena) to stand for complex sets of ideas and emotions. Such symbols function as bases for meditation and reflection, taking on the characteristics of epiphanies. They are very important in religions and in the arts.

We noted that symbols are sometimes understood to differ from signs by being learned and arbitrary. This is true of the use of symbol to refer to words, diagrams, and the like, but it is not true of "symbol" in the sense just described which is important to religion and the arts. Symbols as evocative, resonant items in human consciousness, seem to have some universal significances in addition to whatever is learned. Thus it seems to be possible to write dictionaries of universal symbolism, even while noting that particular religions or cultures emphasize certain elements and omit others. Trees have been prominent as symbols in the arts and religions. For example, in Buddhism a tree is associated with the Buddha's enlightenment; in Christianity with the cross, death, and resurrection. In many cultures trees are symbols of life, either eternal (evergreen) or periodically reviving (deciduous). There are obvious differences but also a common thread of experience and interpretation of trees.

Carl Jung based much of his analysis of human religion and artistic creativity on the theory that such common symbol patterns are given in the basic nature of humanity, its collective unconsciousness. It is not the symbols as they appear to particular cultures and persons but the unconscious predispositions to manifest such symbols that Jung assumed to exist in every human being. These predispositions to certain symbolizations he called "archetypes." Other people use the same word without the particular aspects of Jung's theory in order to name the perennial, apparently basic and important, symbols that keep cropping up in culture after culture, often without any historical connection. Archetype is also used to refer to the models or prototypes in Plato's thought and in some scholastic theology.

Of course there are also things called symbols which are not at all universal. They are drawn from the classical texts, art, oral tradition, and lore of particular cultural traditions. They can be quite powerful in these cultures by providing some commonplaces of imagery, leitmotivs through the centuries, and continuing inspiration to artistic and religious minds. For example, the symbol of God and kings as shepherds is prominent in Hebrew and Christian symbolism, but would not make much sense to traditions without flocks of sheep. It seems to me, however, that most influential symbols do owe some measure of their fascination to universal possibilities in human existence, no matter how local and particular their specific manifestations. Thus, even symbolic patterns that first seem unique to a tradition, like the triune deity of Christian theology, are found to have similarities with patterns in other religions and cultures, e.g., the god triad of Brahman, Vishnu, and Shiva in Hinduism; and the three fates in Greek mythology.

At the most limited level it should also be recognized that there is a purely private realm of symbols. Symbol here functions as a name for items that exist primarily within an individual consciousness, as dreams or personal associations. Other people do not necessarily share the symbolic values that our childhood homes and their furnishings, or crucial incidents in our adolescence, have for each of us. The creative writer often shares his or her private symbolism, and in so doing, enriches our common symbolic life. The author and the religious creator share this function of making their vision of things available to others and they contribute symbols to the common fund. Dublin means so much more to the reader of Joyce's *Ulysses* because his idiosyncratic associations with it have become public in his novel, but it also means other things to other residents and visitors and that remains private.

Because symbols are powerful elements in the experience of many people, they have tended to be described in extravagant language. They are called magic portals, links to eternal truths, and other phrases that highlight their hierophanic character. From a less religious point of view, for instance in the analysis of poetry or the other arts, the power of symbols can be understood in terms of their openendedness, the fascinating links of association they can inspire, and their metaphorical breadth.

The idea that an item is a symbol on the basis of its evocative power in human memory places the specifically symbolic function in the eye of the beholder rather than in the thing itself. For example, a tree in the desert may be just a sign that water is available there. The same tree, however, can symbolize a great deal to someone who reflects on it or has deep associations with it (as a specific plant, a species, or simply a tree). It all depends on the point of view, cultural heritage, and personal experience of the spectator. It takes effort and study to see other peoples' symbols as they see them, even though there is often some common human experience or archetype upon which to draw for empathetic understanding.

People will tend to call those items symbols which inspire and reveal, or have done so in the past. Many such items, however, exist in our talk and writing, without any of the glory or power they may at other times have evoked. These might be called depleted symbols if they have gone completely out of significant use, or maybe they are just latent or potential symbols. This leads to a consideration of a common use of symbol to mean a nonverbal item of communication which stands for quite easily known words or concepts. An example of this kind of symbol would be the red and white striped barber pole which marked the barber's shop in the days when many people who needed to find him could not read. Even though this is a very common way of understanding symbol, I have left its discussion to this point in order to show how different it is from the notions of symbol which approach the idea of epiphanic power. We do not comprehend what religious people and students of religion mean when they talk about the power and importance of symbols if we take them to mean merely word substitutes. Some of these designs are quite common, like the cross to identify a church or the trident to identify Shiva or Poseidon. Even such simple identification symbols can assume revelatory power, but for the most part they are trivial symbols or signs.

After such a long and involved analysis of symbol a summary is in order. I have suggested that most of the meanings of this word can be collected into two major categories: first, where all communication devices including words but not including mere signals are called symbols, and second, where only important, evocative items in human consciousness are called symbols. In addition there are two minor categories of usage: the very general application of the term to all items of communication including signals, and the very narrow application wherein a symbol is a non-verbal item by which to indicate or identify something otherwise clearly known and verbally expressable.

Having tried to bring order into the welter of ways "symbol" is used an equally difficult task lies before us in sorting out the meanings of another key term in religious language, "myth." Probably the most immediate meaning of myth for contemporary English speakers is something false. Newspaper headlines, lecture titles, and similar concise communications often encapsulate arguments as the contrast of fact versus myth. In such statements, however, there is also the assumption that such a myth is not an obvious mistake or an analytical falsehood. That is, one would not say that two plus two equals five is a myth. Instead, the assumption made in using myth is that someone believes the myth even though it is deemed false by the speaker or writer. That social situation is implied in all the uses of the term; it is always used of things believed or accepted as true by some but not by others. It is very rare for someone to use myth of his or her own ideas or beliefs but that is quit odd and not understood by most people. Various definitions and uses of myth" do not stop there, however, but add other more specific notions to the general one of someone else's mis-beliefs. These added meanings can be classified under three headings: form, function, and content.

The question of the form of myth centers on whether it is to be limited to narrative or story. This seems to be the older notion of the word but recently people have wanted to extend the significance of myth beyond strictly narrative materials. They have included all kinds of statements and beliefs which are associated with the old stories called myths. Perhaps it is better to use the adjectival form in this situation, referring to "mythic consciousness" or "mythic thought" which is presupposed by the myth stories. In any event myth is extended in these uses to the supposed mental patterns or conceptions of people who tell and believe myths.

The question of form is not answered completely by reference to narrative, however, because not all narratives are called myths. One needs to determine just what stories qualify as myths by comparison with legend, epic, folktale, and any number of other kinds of stories. First, one notices that myth is usually used of traditional stories, told and retold within a culture. It is characteristically oral literature to which the written form is secondary; a myth is not fixed in wording or even in content but usually exists in variant forms. Myth is also usually applied to stories of indeterminate age and anonymous authorship, although a written version of a myth might be identified with a particular period of history or a named author.

All these qualifications of form are insufficient, however, without some reference to function. What really distinguishes the stories called myths from all others has to do with the importance they have for people. Only those stories (or belief patterns) are considered to be myths which are held to be significant, true, and illuminating. This is the distinction with which we began this analysis of myth and it needs further explication now in a more positive light. Even though the speaker might use myth of things he or she does not hold to be true, the student of religions is interested in learning more about why and how those other people do take their myths to be true. It is usually assumed that myths are important and serious matters for the people who tell and believe them because the myths explain something otherwise unknown or mysterious. Myths can function, by this view, to account for the origin and character of everything from the whole world or the pantheon, to some little detail of nature or culture like the name of a place.

The explanatory function of myths has given rise to various conceptions of or attitudes toward myths among students of this literature. Sometimes myths are seen to be a kind of proto-science or the attempt to understand the world which is later replaced by science. From other viewpoints, however, it seems that scientific knowledge does not replace all myths or all aspects of myths, because the myths explain more than natural phenomena or empirical matters. For example, some of the less appreciative or respectful analyses of primitive thought have been based on the assumption that people in such cultures did not know the facts of human reproduction. It is theorized that people invented myths about the derivation of souls from trees and stones in order to account for conception. It may well be, however, that a deeper mystery was being addressed in these myths, a mystery which modem knowledge of conception, genetics, and cell-division does not resolve or explain, namely the origin and character of all organic life. Even if some particular etiological stories reflect outmoded worldviews, it is not necessarily the case that all myths are dispensable or unimportant.

Perhaps it is better to describe the functional aspect of myth in different terms. Instead of likening the myths to scientific laws or theories, one could see them, or at least some of them, as similar in function to metaphysical and theological assertions, dealing with abstractions and basic principles. They might still be replaceable by other theories, axioms, and faiths when seen in this context, but they will not be dismissed as facilely. Certainly the people who tell and treasure traditional stories often do so with the sense that something important about themselves and the world is revealed and continues to be revealed in them.

An examination of the contents or topics of myths can also

be helpful in the definition of myth. Some students of religion have used a very simple definition based on the cast of characters in a story. Disregarding anything about the function or truth of myths they have settled for a more surface discrimination: Any traditional story that is primarily about gods is a myth. This enables one to distinguish between myths and epics (or legends), both of which may have gods or spirits among their characters but which are primarily about human beings. This is a handy distinction to use on occasion but it ignores some of the most interesting things we might want to say about myths. Certainly some epics and legends have functioned like myths insofar as they have had the importance and revelatory power for some people described above. The close identification of myths with creation myths or the time before time is similarly limiting, even though one might reasonably argue that creation myths are classical examples of the type and must be taken into consideration in any examination of myths.

The term "creation myth" is not quite exact as a name for the whole category of these classical examples of myths. It would be better to call them "origin myths" because this would include stories about any beginning of the world in addition to those involving a creator. In some cultures the world begins with sexual reproduction, in others from a primeval egg, an earth-diver, or a sacrifice. All of these themes and more can be found in the origin myths of various cultures, but their common theme is the beginnings of the natural and the super-natural world. In this kind of story people find out the basic purpose and character of the world, humanity, and everything else there is.

There is another subject matter of myths that is very common which continues from the very first origins of things to deal with their subsequent modification. It seems that origin stories which portray the absolute beginning of the world do not quite account for the world the way it is now, according to the myth-tellers of most traditions. Thus we have an identifiable group of myths which can be thought of as adjustment or change myths. In these stories something about the world and life as first given is adjusted or modified. Many of these stories tell about the origin of death for human beings. They might also at the same time account for the origin of sexuality, for it is fairly clear that one does not have to reproduce if one does not die. In this class of change stories can be placed the stories of "culture-heroes" who initiate various aspects of human culture, from the introduction of fire with which to cook food, to various arts and crafts. The distinctly human aspects of life are often seen to originate in this second kind of myth, as if to say that human culture demands a different stage and type of origination from the rest of the world.

As there are myths that talk about the origin of things so there are myths that portray the end. They are named by transferring the Greek word *eschaton* into English. It refers to the farthest place, the last item in a series, or the last point of time. Eschatalogical myths have been especially important in the Western religions, going back to the influence of Zoroastrianism. This long tradition sees the world as a battleground between good and evil, so the outcome of this contest is important. The Hindu notions of time and history, despite their cyclical character and tremendous numbers, still have stories about the end of the ages and the ultimate end of the world, but without the Zoroastrian intensity which permeates the West. In some other bodies of mythology too there are eschatalogical elements. Religious groups for which this kind of myth is the most central and determinative are called "millennialist," from the thousand-year period in Christian eschatologies. It has been noted that an overarching concern with eschatological myth is characteristic of oppressed peoples, those for whom the present state of affairs politically and culturally is very unsatisfactory. It is easy to understand that they might cherish myths that express their hope for significant change in the future.

There is a special genre of literature which expresses eschatological mythology called "apocalyptic." An apocalypse characteristically describes the end of the world and events leading up to it in an allegorical fashion, with extravagant imagery. In the Western religions the end of the world is heralded by the arrival of a significant human or semi-human figure. Although other people could be anointed and thus be messiahs in Hebrew-Jewish theology, messiah was adopted by Christianity and became the basic word for this future agent of God. Christians and Muslims expect Jesus to return; this is sometimes called the second coming or *parousia*. The Muslims also speak of the *mahdi* as an eschatological figure.

These three categories of myth topics all share the characteristic of being set in a time which is not historical, at least by most senses of that word. The time of origin and change myths takes place before the world as we know it appears, and the time of eschatalogical myths is usually assumed to be in the future. Cyclic eschatologies, of course, take place at the end of each era or cycle. "Realized eschatology" refers to the idea that the end of the world may have taken place already but has not been noticed or not fully realized yet.

History, as a word and a category, is usually reserved for the accounts of those events which have taken place in the world as we know it, the human world of the past which is continuous with the present. More must be said about history later but it is sufficient at this point to note that for many people history and myth are mutually exclusive. From this perspective, if an account or story of the supposed past (or future) centers on human beings pretty much like us and in a time and place pretty much like ours, it cannot be called "myth." It must be put in another category, like epic, legend, science fiction, etc. However, some histories function in the ways that myths function, even if they are not called myths. If such stories about the human past are thought to be true, important, and deserving of constant rehearsal and reference; and if such stories are ritually celebrated and studied for their implications for theology and ethics; then they might as well be called myths.

With these considerations in mind it seems meaningful to

some to class the treasured historical accounts of many religious traditions in the category of myth, despite the problems that arise when other dimensions of the word, namely the associations of being fictitious and false, bring pejorative attitudes into play. Many people might jump to the conclusion that if an historical account is called a myth it is also being declared a complete fabrication. This is not the case, however, for there are people who do not use myth in this sense when calling historical accounts myths. What these people want to say is actually not an accusation of falsehood but a way of respecting such stories. Calling some histories myths attempts to say that, whatever the historical accuracy of these stories, they are treasured as more than mere records of the past. Instead they are cherished as meaningful, important, revelatory stories. Perhaps it is usually the case that such mythical histories contain some measure of elaboration and enhancement. This happens in the reverent traditional transmission of the stories in which accuracy in preserving historical detail is not as important as the expression of wonder and allegorical elaboration. In fact it becomes an identifying hallmark of histories functioning mythically that the marvelous and the meaningful expand the mere event. There is no reason, however, why a perfectly accurate and verifiable (insofar as history is ever verifiable) historical account cannot become mythic for a community or even an individual for whom it is deeply significant.

Within the category of historical myth, then, one can place the story of the exodus from Egypt that dominated the recorded memory of the ancient Israelites and the story of the life of Jesus which is at the center of Christianity. Stories of the lives of the Buddha or Muhammad are less central to their traditions but still important. When we apply the terms of religion study to the analysis of national consciousness, which some people are willing to call "civil religion," the mythic function of historical accounts is also unmistakable. George Washington and the other heroes of the American Revolution are the subject of much mythology in this sense. More recent examples could also be cited, although when people create myth deliberately we might wish to call it propaganda or ideology rather than mythology. One might theorize that even if Nazi cultivation of Teutonic traditional stories was self-conscious on the part of a few, it was myth, with its old power and aura, for many in the general population.

Of course there are other ways of classifying myths other than by their subject matter, topic, or theme. One can, for example, develop a classification based on the area of life or nature that is apparently explained by the myth, such as nature, social structure, or the individual psyche. There is a lot of selection and interpretation on the part of the classifier in this kind of division of mythology; and that should be admitted and self-conscious lest other meanings and uses of a myth be ignored. Some of the most famous myths cannot be so easily classified because they have had applications and transformations involving many aspects of life. In fact, it might be said to be characteristic of people who find myths valuable that they apply them to all areas of life, and in those applications unify their worldview.

Many words have come up in the discussion of myth which are not as difficult but which deserve a bit of attention, "epic," "legend," "parable," and "allegory." Epic is usually applied to those stories whose list of characters contain human beings primarily, despite any incidental appearance of the gods or other supernatural elements, and which recount the supposed events surrounding the establishment of a nation or a people. The sweep and scope of such stories are often so grand that the term has been appropriated for film advertisement as an indicator of high drama on a large scale. The classical epics of the world have been important as the myths of national identity, and have also had more specifically religious influence in providing stories for imitation and celebration in religious traditions. The importance of the Mahabharata for Hinduism or the Iliad for ancient Greece can hardly be over-estimated. Both epics and many more may have been based on historical events to some extant but this historicity is difficult to establish and is ultimately irrelevant to the reasons why people cherish them. Epics might be classified as historical myths or as traditional literature that sometimes has great importance to a culture or nation. Legend is often used for less grand, long, or revered stories of presumed history.

The problem of truth or historicity is rarely at issue in stories called parables. Most people would not worry about whether parables were fictional or not because the word implies that the narrative exists as illustration of a point or principle and is not to be taken out of the context of the teaching or preaching situation in which it is embedded. Fables like those of Aesop are of the same order in that they are usually understood to be little fictions from which a lesson is to be derived. The parables of Jesus in the New Testament are classic examples of this type of literature and their analysis has often emphasized that these parables are oriented toward one basic point or are the development of one central metaphor. This distinguishes parables from allegories, because the latter term is used for stories which have many points of reference to a parallel set of ideas. Many of the parables in the New Testament are really allegories from this perspective, and some scholars have conjectured that this is due to an allegorizing tendency in the circles of disciples who preserved the parables of Jesus. Whoever did the allegorizing, such an elaborate story structure, with its explicit or implicit interpretation, is a more complex form of the parable, which in turn can be seen as a complex form of a metaphor.

More could be said about words for the words in religions, of course, but these paragraphs have covered some of the most problematic areas dealing with communication in general. Next we must examine the words for religious verbal activities of a written and more formal sort.

9 | THEOLOGY AND
RELIGIOUS LITERATURE

The words in this chapter concern the more formal side of religious language, the propositions and arguments of theology as a scholarly discipline. This discussion merges into a consideration of written religious literature because the study of texts is so important a part of theological work. Religious texts and theological activity might be based on myths and symbols which existed previously in oral or picture form, in which case they may be thought to be derivative expressions. In other cases, however, writing and theologizing might be themselves basic, originative religious phenomena, independent of stories or other religious activity. In other words, there will be a difference among scholars and among believers in their evaluation of both texts and theology because some will look through the text and the system of thought for the basic myth, symbol, or experience, while others will find in the text and the doctrine the holy or revelatory itself.

"Theology" literally means words about god, but it has come to apply also to religious statements about subjects other than god. Some people use it loosely to refer to all talk about religious matters, in which case it would include both the perspectives from inside and outside a stance of religious commitment. It has seemed more appropriate to many people, however, to restrict "theology" to the kind of religious discussion which takes place within a circle of faith or belief. Theology, in this usage, refers to a number of intellectual activities in which members of a religious group engage, either singly or collectively. The thoughts and statements of theology in this restricted sense presuppose acceptance of the basic symbols and documents of a religious tradition, and assume a continuity with the past as well as with other believers in the present. A person who is not a believer in a religion can, with sufficient background, think and write as if he or she were part of the tradition and even contribute to its theological tradition, but this is rare. Usually theological activity is the conversation of believers with each other and towards outsiders, and it is based in the life of a believing community with all the other elements in addition to study and thought that comprise the religious situation.

Theologies and religious groups are sometimes characterized according to their styles of thought, which may or may not be deemed praiseworthy by the user of the word. Some theologies are called "orthodox," because they make a point of being close to the old customs and ideas of their traditions. The word is derived from roots that mean right opinion. Those who hold another opinion or set of doctrines may be called "heterodox" or "heretic" (see Chapter 5). Some theologies are called "fundamentalist," a term which was coined in America by people who wanted to reject innovations in Christianity and return to the fundamentals of their religion. The fundamentalist position is especially identified by the assertion of inerrancy in the Bible. This means that every statement in the Bible must be taken as a statement of fact, including historical and physical matters. By extension fundamentalist can be used of certain movements in other religions which deal with their religious traditions in a comparable way. Some theologies are said to be "scholastic" which means that they are especially formal or logical. By contrast with these terms some theologies are called "liberal," but that does not say very much specifically, only that such theologies are understood to be free of some or all of these and other constraints.

The propositions or statements about reality in a theological system are called "doctrines" or "dogmas." The latter word, especially in the adjectival form "dogmatic," has come to be associated with rigidity in one's position, and indeed many believers have tolerated little or no flexibility regarding their theological statements. It is not inevitable, however, that a doctrine be anything more than its etymology implies, namely, a teaching. Teachings are accepted on the authority of a teacher or teaching institution which may or may not be given absolute allegiance, and thus they can be understood in less absolute terms than dogma connotes.

Another noteworthy aspect of religious conviction or commitment is that doctrines are accepted or rejected pretty much as a package. Sometimes this package is called a "theological circle," that is, an inter-related series of ideas which imply each other and should be treated as a group. Certainly theologians in any religion argue over details but recognize a common commitment to the basic propositions, at least until the diversity seems intolerable, at which point a new religious group or identity may be formed. Otherwise they maneuver within a given circle of presuppositions and propositions which is distinct from any other religion or school of thought. Statements made within such a circle may not mean much, if anything, outside it.

There are a number of subdivisions within the general category of theology. "Systematic theology" names the attempts made to collect and explain in orderly fashion the various doctrines and assumptions of a religious group, mainly for the edification of its professional leadership and other interested members. "Natural theology" refers to the propositions of a theological system which its theologians assume is understandable and logical to everyone, whether a member of the religious tradition or not. Some people think that there is much natural theology, including the doctrines of the existence of God and of a moral order, but others think the category is empty or close to it.

The term "apology" (or "apologetics") has been used to

designate theological activity geared mainly toward outsiders. The apologetic task is to explain the beliefs of the religious group in a way that is understandable to outsiders, in the hopes of tolerance and perhaps sympathy. By contrast some theological activity is geared to the persuasion or conversion of the outsider and that should be distinguished from the apologetic task. "Evangelization" refers to the theological activity which aims at incorporation of the recipient into the group and affirmation of its beliefs. "Evangelism" and related words are Christian terms derived from Greek roots which mean a good message. They can be used to refer to similar activity in other religions, but proselytizing and missionary activity are probably more common words in non-Christian contexts. Certainly every religious group thinks that its view of the world is ultimately beneficial, no matter how negative some of its positions might seem to be from an outsider's point of view. Thus we can expect to find apologetic and proselytizing activity in every religious group that comes into contact with others. "Preaching" is not always directed toward outsiders. Addresses to the faithful are called "sermons" or "homilies," the latter being characteristically shorter or less rhetorically developed than the former.

Another type of theological activity is called "catechetics." This refers to the traditional form of teaching the young or the newlyconverted Christians which was by the recitation of pre-scribed questions and answers. Catechism more broadly refers to any instructions in the rudiments of a religion. Such teaching is often centered on some basic formulation of the faith called a "creed" from the Latin *credo*, I believe. The three refuges in Buddhism and the *shahadah* of Islam, while shorter, are compa-rable to the Christian creeds as indications of the *sine qua non* of their respective religions. These summary commitment statements are often used in ritual contexts. Although the term "confession" can be used to refer to the statements one makes about one's acts, as in a confession of sins, confession is also used for a statement of belief, as in "The Augsburg Confession," a summary statement of the positions of the Lutheran reformers. Such statements or collections of such statements are also sometimes called "symbols," perhaps with reference to the notion that a symbol is a means of identification, here identifying a system of belief. Many words associated with the activity of theology are concerned with reading and interpretation of sacred texts. As long as a religious tradition is oral its theology is rudimentary and is expressed mainly in hymns and myths. When these and other verbal forms are written down, however, these writings, especially the most revered of them, take on a special importance. Much theological energy is then devoted to the understanding of these texts. Commentaries are written which attempt to explain, amplify, and apply the older texts.

When some revered texts become the classics of their tradition, that is, the texts which most people in a religious group read, refer to, and trust, they are said to become "canonical." Derived from a root meaning rule and standard, canon has many applications in religious history. Here it designates a watershed in religious literature between the ordinary, no matter how much respected, and the sacred. That line may be formally recognized, or may be somewhat fluid and adjustable. The words "Scripture" and "Bible" display this ambiguity in that etymologically they merely mean writings and books, but have come to mean the writings and the books, that is, the sacred ones.

The writings which might have been included in the various Jewish and Christian canons, but were not, have been called "apocrypha," which means hidden books. The groups of writings most often referred to by this term are those Jewish books written in Greek which were not included in the Jewish canon at the end of the first century CE. This Greek Jewish collection is called the Septuagint (abbreviated LXX) from the legend that it was produced by 70 translators. Protestant Bibles relegate these disputed writings to secondary status under the name apocrypha, but they are included in the Vulgate, the Latin translation of the Bible, which is the standard for Roman Catholicism. Even there they are sometimes labeled "deutero-canonical" or second level canon. There is also a New Testament apocrypha consisting of early Christian writings not included in the canon which gained acceptance by most Christian communities in the first three centuries CE.

A second level of non-canonical religious writings are those which were rarely even under consideration to be canonical but have great prestige nevertheless. In Christianity this would be the status of the writings ascribed to the church fathers or patristic writings, as well as various creedal statements. Judaism has a large literature of this type collected under the name "talmud." There are two such collections, the Babylonian and the Jerusalem or Palestinian, which contain *mishnah*, originally oral comments of Jewish law, plus *gemorah* or *gemara*, which is commentary on *mishnah*. Talmud merely means learning and thus "talmudic" can be used loosely to refer to the whole period of classic rabbinic scholarship.

Another term for a category of semi-Biblical writings is "pseudepigrapha." These writings are important for historians and students of the ancient religious texts but are not canonical or theologically authoritative for prevailing religious groups. They may have had influence and authority in ancient religious groups and could theoretically have such again, but today these miscellaneous writings are background reading for academic study only. The name means false superscription and refers to the pervasive ancient practice of false ascriptions of authorship. The real writers are anonymous, having chosen to say that their words are due to some prominent figure in the history of their tradition. This category can overlap with apocrypha, in part depending on the canon one uses.

Other religious traditions illustrate this same layering of canonicity, that is, there is often a category of writings between the sacred and the ordinary. Islam's canon consists clearly of the Qur'an. Where the Qur'an does not provide precedent or guidance in thought and practice, however, the Muslim turns to the *sunnah* of the prophet Muhammad, his words and deeds as recorded in *hadith*. The various collections of *hadith* are quite extensive compared to the relative brevity of the Qur'an, and provide full-time work for the Muslim scholars in evaluating and applying each tradition. The *hadith* are not as authoritative as the Qur'an but definitely more important than any other religious writings.

Hindus divide their authoritative texts into the "shruti," hearing, and "smirti," memory. The first is more sacred and consists of the Veda *samhitas* or collections, beginning with the Veda hymns and ending with the Upanishads, the vedanta or end of the Vedas. As usual, the second category, smirti, is much larger and in this case somewhat open-ended. It certainly includes the great epics, the Mahabharata and the Ramayana, but also texts known as Puranas, old stories, and the law-books, e.g. that of Manu. The Bhagavad Gita, which is a part of the Mahabharata, has a prominent role in its own right. Beyond these texts there is an ocean of religious literature both in Sanskrit, the Indo-European language of the writings mentioned above, and in later dialects and in Dravidian languages. These can have great popularity and status among various Hindu groups.

Buddhism's canon is clear as far as the Theravada tradition is concerned. This branch of Buddhism, also called Hinayana and based on texts in Pali, a Sanskritic language, gives canonical status to a body of writings known collectively as the Tripitaka or three baskets. The Mahayana side of Buddhism presents us with a much less precise canonical situation. Among the various sects under this umbrella name there are an extraordinarily large number of writings or "sutras." In each sect some few sutras will have, in effect, canonical status, and the rest might serve as do the secondary collections we have noted in other traditions, as advanced reading for the professional.

In China, in addition to the Buddhism and its texts, there are two major literary traditions, the Confucian and the Taoist. For the former and basic to all Chinese culture the canon is the five classics: the Books are 1-Documents or History, 2-Songs or Poetry, 3-Manners or Rituals, 4-Changes, and 5-the Spring and Autumn Annals. In the secondary category there are four more classics including the Analects of Confucius. The Taoist tradition centers on the Tao-te-Ching, but based on the model of the Buddhist Tripitaka the Taoists established a basket of sacred writings which is quite extensive.

These are not the only religions or traditions with sacred writings and canons, but these are some of the major examples of the phenomenon. The religions are different from each other, of course, so their texts will also differ in content and character. Within most of these collections of sacred writings, furthermore, there is a great variety of styles and modes of writing. Granted that some, like the Qur'an, are fairly uniform in character, most canons contain materials from many eras and situations, with many literary genres involved. These forms of writing may characterize a whole unit or it may be an element in the midst of other styles of writing. As usual we cannot be exhaustive in our list but we can develop an alertness to such variety of genres by mentioning a few.

The term "apocalyptic" has been noted a few times, especially in connection with eschatological mythology. This is a literary form with some clear defining elements. It is written as the report of a vision or dream on the part of the author, often pseudonymous. The vision displays realities of the normally unseen, trans-human world, and often describes events of history, culminating in a dramatic set of future events. Its language by any standard is bizarre and the symbolism rife. The Greek *apokalyptein* means to uncover or reveal; thus the New Testament example of the genre is known as the Apocalypse or Revelation. Though it is used first of Western religious writings, the term can be applied to similar writings elsewhere.

Other genres of canonical writing include forms obviously rooted in ritual practice. Among these are hymns and poetry, ritual directions or rubrics (based on the Latin for red since they were written or printed in that color), sermons, formulas of blessing and cursing, and words used in meditation. Then there are materials that may not have been written with ritual context in mind. These include stories of all kinds including histories, theological explanations and defences, catechetical materials, sayings and speeches of famous people, essays and poetry, letters, prophecies and oracles, legal or moral injunctions, and commentaries on any of the above. The important point, of course, is to recognize the variety of materials and approach each text with respect for its basic form and function.

Religious and secular scholarship usually insists on using the original languages and original words of the canonical and semi-canonical writings. Translations are called "versions" and are usually understood to have value and authority only insofar as they represent the meanings of the original language. Versions can take on authority in their own right, however, as has the King James Version of the Christian Bible among some English-speaking Protestant groups. The Latin Vulgate has also had influence in Roman Catholicism as an authority itself, beyond its role as a translation. Scholars have also been attentive to the various copies of the ancient texts, especially of the original languages but also of the versions. Since ancient texts before printing had to be copied by hand variations and errors occurred. At many points in religious history the bad copies of a sacred text were destroyed, but there are often very old variant readings, and an elaborate scholarly task is involved in sorting and judging the various possibilities.

Instead of examining the words and languages of the texts, scholarship may take other directions in the validation of sacred writings. Archeological evidence, other written materials from the surrounding cultures, chemical analysis of papers, skins, and other artifacts, all can play a role in religious scholarship as well as in academic study outside the circles of religious conviction. These are fairly modem practices; there have been other traditional techniques as well. The Islamic process of verifying *hadiths*, for example, concentrates on the line of transmission from a contemporary of Muhammad to the written form of the *sunnah*. *Hadiths* are accepted or rejected on the basis of the character and reputation of the people whose names appear in the list of transmitters.

All the techniques and principles of interpretation are gathered under the name "hermeneutics." We have reviewed many of its activities, like the analysis of forms, oral and written. These sub-disciplines are sometimes known as form criticism and source criticism, the search for the background to the present form of a text. The term criticism here does not mean negative comment, as in common parlance, but unjudgmental investigation. Hermeneutical activity centers on the process known as "exegesis," the reading of correct meaning out of a text. *Midrash* is a Hebrew word for the same thing, being derived from a root that means, to investigate or inquire.

The alternative to exegesis, namely reading meaning into a text rather than out of it, is sometimes given its correlative Greek-English form, *eisegesis*. Whether it is named or not, that is the perennial temptation or opportunity. People love to find or uncover obscure and hidden interpretations which, from another point of view, may well be, or at least look like, distortions of the text's original meaning. A step in clarifying this situation is taken when exegetes distinguish between literal meanings and all others, not necessarily rejecting the others as illegitimate. These other interpretations can range from fairly obvious implications of the literal meaning to a treatment of the text as if it were a code. Interpretation of a text as if it were a code is based on the assumption that the text is really trying to communicate something quite different than its apparent meaning. This hidden message must be read by means of a special deciphering of the literal text.

Having a sacred text, widely known and distributed, can be an advantage to a religious tradition in preserving continuity in theological discussion over centuries and miles. There is also a major disadvantage, however, in the limits it places on change. This is a disadvantage if the human situation changes. It is not necessary to say that change is always good to realize that it seems to be inevitable in the course of human history. For some religious people it is impious to say that the sacred texts may need any adjustment, but it is fairly obvious to other believers and outside observers that even the most respected of sacred texts must bow to the necessity of change, one way or another.

Within the hermeneutical artillery of theologians there are a number of devices for accomplishing changes without departing disrespectfully from the words of the sacred texts. Primary among these devices is allegory. If it can be assumed that a religious text does not mean exactly or at all what it says on the surface, but that it conceals another set of ideas, then a great deal can be incorporated into the tradition under the guise of new interpretations of the ancient words. Another way in which change takes place occurs when a commentator applies the text to a new situation by generalizing from the particular items in the text. Of course it is also possible in many traditions for clearly new doctrines to be added to those expressed or implied in the sacred texts, in which case the problem is not as acute.

What we have surveyed so far deals with the role of texts in theology. They also have ritual and magical applications. Bibles and other religious texts have been treated very reverentially in many situations. The physical documents themselves, as well as the reading of them, may have ceremonial elaboration. They may be used as the Bible has been in American courtrooms and civic ceremonies, as a holy item by or on which to swear honesty or make a vow. There is also a kind of resort to the texts which consists of opening the volume at random and pointing at a passage. The selected words are thought to be a particular message for the moment. This is called "stichomancy" or *sortes sanctorum* in Latin.

This concludes our summary of the study of religious writings. All the disciplines and terms in this chapter may be theological, faith-based activities, but many can be undertaken without religious commitment in an attempt to understand peoples and their history for the sake of such understanding alone. The next chapter moves beyond the strictly theological and the area of overlap between religious and academic study, and enters into the terminology used more often from the analytical, secular perspective.

10 | GOD LANGUAGE

The words and conceptions connected with gods and other supernatural beings present us with an interesting analytical challenge. There are so many words and they have overlapping meanings! Therefore, I shall undertake my survey in a way which may be unusual, by seeing all the words we are about to review as a group. This grouping consists of all the beings above and beyond human beings and nature. By examining them in this context, each term can be placed roughly in a scale from slightly to absolutely super-human or super-natural. The place in the scale will depend on each word's associations with other words in the group. This may seem strange at first, but I think that it will serve to clarify usage even if it does not correspond immediately with various doctrinal statements.

The most general and ambiguous word for this group is "spirit." Spirit is based on words for breath and air like other words in this category: Greek *pneuma*, Hebrew *ruach*, Latin *anima*, with their English derivatives. It identifies a special aspect or part of human beings as well as the non-human beings. As a synonym for "soul" it will be reviewed later in connection with religious words and ideas concerning human beings. As a word for beings in the realm of the super-human it can apply to minor sprites, elves, and the like, all the way up to the great spirits of Zoroastrianism and the Holy Spirit of Christianity. The essential characteristics of anything called spirit would seem to be non-physicality or invisibility, coupled with power or potential influence. Neither it nor the adjective spiritual say anything very specific, and are thus best used when little which is specific can or should be said.

From the point of view of many religions it is arbitrary and inappropriate to differentiate as clearly as this book does between living and dead human beings because the dead are merely the same beings in a different phase of life. Nevertheless, some consideration of words and ideas for dead human beings must be undertaken here in the chapter on gods while also mentioning them later in connection with words and ideas for live human beings. In some theologies the difference between humanity and deity is a matter of degree, and many conceptions of the role and power of ancestors and the dead are indistinguishable from notions concerning non-human spirits and gods.

"Ghost" is an example of a word with that range of meanings. Older Christian English usage permitted Holy Ghost as a synonym for Holy Spirit, but perhaps it is the Halloween associations of ghost that have shifted preference to the latter. Despite the more general application of the German cognate, *Geist*, the word ghost has moved to the human end of the whole field of meaning. There is fear and reverence for the hungry ghosts of Tibetan and Chinese lore and the ancestors which remain somehow in touch with the world of the living in many traditions. They are treated like the gods are treated in other places. The customs of Halloween in the United States are a secularized version of a widespread ritual pattern in which the ghosts or ancestors return to the realm of the living at a certain time of the year. They must be given gifts, especially food, or they will harm the living, hence the mantra: trick or treat.

The words "god," "goddess," and their plurals are rarely used for human beings but can be used for anything in the total realm of the super-human from minor figures in a pantheon to an absolute deity. The multitude of gods, *devas* and *ashuras* in the Hindu tradition, for example, seem to be more like the angels or spirits in other theologies. That is, they are often thought to occupy a position between human beings and the ultimate being or power of the universe. In Hinduism this absolute god is usually named "Brahman" or "the One." God is a generic term in English for all these beings, but it is also used in the Western religions as a major word for referring to the one ultimate being, both in academic and religious discussion. Because of its religious use some people treat it reverentially by avoiding its pronunciation in non-religious situations or writing it "G-d." This word and others in this category are often capitalized as a sign of respect or as a proper name.

"Deity" is perhaps the least religious of the words for gods. It is usually used in contexts where piety is not present or desired, for example, abstract philosophical discussion. Appropriately, a philosophical religion popular in the eighteenth century is called "Deism." Although this movement posited a creator god and a moral order it did not encourage ritual or experiential recognition of that god. Deity is based on a Latin root, as is "divinity," also a fairly abstract word for the god category.

Many other words in the vocabulary for the super-human are based on the Greek cognate *theos*. "Theism" in its broader sense refers to any belief in any kind of god and is thus an antonym for atheism. There is a narrower use of the word, however, that restricts it to belief in personal gods. This is an important distinction. It makes a big difference in theologies whether their god is thought to be somewhat like human beings or entirely different from them. Obviously few gods, except for the lower types, are limited in vulnerability and mortality as much as human beings are. Power and capability greater than humanity's is a defining characteristic of deity. Personality is another matter, however. Human beings do not always think of it as limiting but often as a major benefit of being human. Personality, philosophically analyzed, however, is not compatible with some of the absolutes ascribed to the highest of the gods.

Let us examine the ramifications of the term "person." It is derived from the Greek word for the mask used by an actor. That so wonderful a phenomenon as personality could be linked to so superficial a notion of identity is probably offensive to many people. This is true especially in the West with its fascination with individuality. By contrast it is a common assumption of Indian theologies that personal identity is not a feature of one's ultimate self. At any rate, personality implies the ability to talk and to respond, capacity for love and growth, individuality and self-consciousness. All these qualities mix poorly if at all with god-notions of omnipotence, omniscience, changelessness, and the like. No matter what the conceptual difficulties, however, theism and theists, using the word in the narrower sense, affirm personality and divinity in one and the same being. Most Christian theologies carry this a step further by affirming three persons in one being, the doctrine of the Trinity.

It is worth noting that personality language seems to be inevitable in myths because stories involve persons. Abstract propositional theology tends to use impersonal or trans-personal language and categories. Sometimes ascription of personality to gods is extended to the association of other human characteristics, even body parts, with gods. This is called "anthropomorphism." It is usually the critics who use this word to make a charge against theists, while the theists argue the metaphorical or analogical character of anthropomorphic terminology. This is a kind of dispute that takes place within self-conscious theological systems.

Another level of the problem of personality and deity occurs in the study of ancient mythologies. The word "personification" has been used in discussions of the connection of gods with natural phenomena. This term implies that earliest human beings recognized impersonal nature and imposed personality upon it. If this was the process it was rather stupid, or perhaps due to a disease of language, as one scholar theorized. Others scholars have reversed this process in their theories of the origin of religion. They assume instead that earliest people saw the world entirely as persons and later demoted certain aspects to the status of personless things.

Words ending in "-theism" vary in the degree to which they maintain the sense of a personal god. "Pantheism," the idea that all is god and god is everything, is an impersonal god notion. "Panentheism" is sometimes used to name a compromise position between theism and pantheism in which god is more than the world but not absolutely transcendent. "Polytheism," the belief in many gods and goddesses, implies personal identities in the society of the gods. "Monotheism" is ambiguous, often used of theistic gods but also more inclusively. A clearly impersonal god notion which also emphasizes oneness and uniqueness can be named "monism." "Henotheism" is also built from roots meaning one god but with the special sense that one god is selected from many to be one's own. This situation is also called "monolatry," which adds the observation that selection of a god from among many results in worshipping that god instead of others. A Hindu (Sanskrit) term for this is *ista-devata*, or chosen deity. The ancient Hebrews seem to have had this notion of worshipping one god to the exclusion of others, and also felt themselves to be chosen for this worship and special responsibility by their god.

Other words using the root *theos* include "pantheon," which means the whole community of the gods in a polytheistic system as well as the building in which they are worshipped, especially the famous pantheon of ancient Rome. "Theodicy" names the problem in philosophy and theology of the suffering and evil in the world. Religions which affirm both the omnipotence and goodness of their god face a problem in accounting for naturally and humanly produced pain. The etymology of theodicy indicates that this is a question of the justice of god. "Theocracy" adds a root for power to god and thus names a political situation in which people understand themselves to be ruled by their god, either through an agent or by divinely revealed laws, or both. Yet other, less frequent, combinations are "theogony," a story of the birth and genealogy of the gods; "theomachy," battle against or among the gods; and "theomorphic," having the form of a god.

All these words are usually taken to be generic for the category of deity. There are also personal names for gods, some of which are so prominent that they should be discussed. Some god names, however, seem to be both generic and personal. The Arabic word *Allah* is used as if it is a proper name for the supreme being in Islam, but etymologically it means simply the god. There are many goddesses in Hindu mythology and ritual, for example Kali, Durga, Lakshmi, and Parvati. These goddesses individually or taken together in some inclusive being are sometimes named and worshipped simply as *Devi*, the goddess, or even more abstractly as *Shakti*, power. Brahman is sometimes used of a personal god and thus like a personal name, but other contexts are impersonal, making it a synonym for the One, the basis of the universe beyond personality. Brahman is an especially confusing word, for it also refers to a number of things in addition to god. Brahmans are a group of people with inherited priestly responsibility. Brahman is associated with the words which they use, and to the power which is in those words. There is also a specific group of ancient texts, usually named by the transliteration Brahmanas so it is distinguishable from the other brahman words in English.

The ancient Israelite proper name of god is called the "tetragrammaton" because it has four letters in Hebrew, transliterated YHWH. In order to avoid disrespect for the name and its referent, the word was not spoken by pious believers, even when it appeared in a sacred text. Instead, a more general but respectful word was used, *adonai*, translated lord but printed LORD in many English Bibles to distinguish this substitution of lord for YHWH from the actual occurrence of *adonai* in the Hebrew. Some Bibles and other publications use "Yahweh," the older English word "Jehovah," or some spelling variation where the tetragrammaton appears in the text.

There was also a generic word for god in ancient Hebrew which exhibits an interesting phenomenon in the words for gods. *Elohim* is grammatically plural but understood to be singular in many but not all contexts. The plural form of *elohim* has been explained as a plural of majesty or royalty based on the logic that a king is not a private person but the focal point of a whole court and nation. Nevertheless, this allows for some ambiguities, like the sons of god or gods in Genesis 6, Job, and some Psalms. There is also a word in the singular for god, *el*, with its own plural *elim*, which is used in other Semitic languages also as the proper name of a particular god.

The chief god of the ancient Greek pantheon was called "Zeus," a word related to generic words for god and sky in Indo-European languages. In the Roman pantheon the comparable god is named "Jupiter" and the ancient Aryans in India had a god *Dyaus Pitri*. In these two cases the root for father is added. Similarly many goddess figures are called "earth mothers" or simply "Mother." These examples illustrate the role of parenting in conceptualizing and naming deities. Other functions can be used to name gods as in those situations where a god is called Creator or Providence. The latter term emphasizes the foresight and care of a personal deity.

Speaking of the functions of gods, we should note that some scholars have classified deities according to their functions. One of these categories is the "culture hero." This is the kind of god who establishes the bases of culture for humankind. These include the introduction of fire, domestication of animals, the discovery of agriculture, and the invention of water-control devices. Comparable, but perhaps better described as dysfunctional is the "trickster" figure who also establishes aspects of the world, but especially aspects which are not so helpful. Another suggestion of this type is the notion of "*dema*-deities," named for figures in the mythology of New Guinea, who have benefited the world by being sacrificed. From their sacrifice, food and other phenomena of the world arise. One theory about Indo-European cultures assumes that they conceived of their pantheon in a pattern of three functions: magisterial, defensive, and productive. The Latin term *deus otiosus*, or English "otiose" has been used to describe a god which no longer has any function at all, usually applied to a creator who ceased to do anything once creation was complete.

Sometimes gods are classified by scholars according to their association with some phenomena of nature. Prominent among these are the "sky-gods." We have seen that Zeus and his counterparts in Indo-European mythologies are associated with the sky. Christians pray to a father in heaven, which is usually thought to be above the sky. "Heaven" and "Lord on high" are terms for a semi-personal god in the Chinese tradition. The sky seems to be an especially appropriate symbol for ultimate reality; many religious traditions locate a powerful deity there

Another classification for gods is based on a slightly lower location, the aerial. These are the gods of planets, stars, and sun, thought to be travelers under the sky in traditional cosmologies. Here also are the storm and rain gods. Finally, terrestrial and sub-terrestrial gods can be put in one group. These are the gods, and especially goddesses, of grain or harvest and the lords of the underworlds.

Even if some aspect of nature or a particular kind of activity name and define many of the deities reviewed above, all of them are considered to be beyond or behind such manifestations. Theologies rarely if ever understand the gods to be nothing more than the natural element or process by which they are identified. Rather it would seem that these gods are understood to be the hidden essence or force of which the more visible phenomenon is a manifestation. This basic notion of invisible deity becoming visible in physical epiphanies is most clearly expressed in a doctrine of incarnation or, using the Hindu term, *avatar*. This is the doctrine of the embodiment of a god in a particular animal or human being. The avatars of the Hindu god Vishnu range from fish and boar, to human or semi-human figures, like Rama, Krishna, and Kalki. According to the myths they appear when the world needs extra assistance, and they become central figures in piety, sometimes even eclipsing Vishnu as the primary form of god. Christianity has a comparable idea in the doctrine of the incarnation. One of the differences between Christianity and the Indian religions lies in the uniqueness of incarnation in Jesus compared to the general doctrine of reincarnation in India, in which context the notion of divine incarnation is less unusual. Another kind of human-god combination is the god who once was human. Unlike the generic ghosts or ancestors who also once were human, there are specific figures, with personal names who become godlike figures in religions. An ancient Hellenistic thinker, Euhemerus, thought all god myths were exaggerated legends of former heroes; therefore this theory regarding the origin of deity and myth is called "Euhemerism." Supporting this are the stories of god-human miscegenation in much mythology, resulting in figures like Hercules. Buddhism exhibits the pattern in the many Buddhas and Bodhisattvas who are thought to have been human and subsequently function like gods, especially in aiding human beings. The saints in some branches of Christianity look like the minor deities in polythesitic pantheons, even in their bureaucratic specializations. Hagiographies or hagiologies, i.e. stories of saints' lives, often feature some element which then becomes the special province of that saint, for example St. George and the military.

Many religions and cultures have ideas of and names for other mysterious beings that populate the world. As with Buddhas and saints we are in a realm of the super-human where "god" is less clearly appropriate but might be used. The Japanese nature forces called *kami* may or may not warrant inclusion in the category god. Some people have used the term "godling" to indicate these ubiquitous nature beings. In Japan and elsewhere such spirits are thought to inhabit trees, springs, and other parts of the natural world. The being who looks like a human being or a son of man in Daniel 7 is another super-human yet not supreme being . The phrase "son of man" took on more meanings as it was associated with the term "messiah" in Christian texts. The ancient Israelite sons of gods belong in this group too.

The word "angel" is used widely to name a kind of being

between human beings and gods in power and significance. The Greek root of the word, meaning "messenger," shows that angels are conceived more as lackeys or agents than powers in their own right. Perhaps traditional imagination could not conceive of great super-human powers not having servants and armies just like powerful human beings. As in human life, however, it would seem to have been expectable also that some servants would be uncooperative or traitorous. Hence the notion of angel-like beings who are unfriendly, like the demons or jinn.

Angels seem to be a difficult category to keep straight. There is some confusion between bad angels and jinn in Islam. In Christian lore dead human beings are confused with angels. In Hebrew texts angel-like beings and god are confused, for example in stories about Jacob (Genesis 32). There is a type of celestial being called "watchers" mentioned in Daniel 4; sometimes these have been considered good angels and sometimes evil. A school of Western religious philosophy, Neoplatonism, placed angels between human beings and god in a great chain of being, making the differences between any of them just a matter of degree. Angeology is a large part of Western religious lore with many categories of angels, some with their own personal names and myths.

Mention above of unfriendly spirits or angels brings us to the consideration of the negatively conceived supernatural beings. Again, there are many words for malevolent spirits. What unites these words is the conception of a kind of super-human being who harms human beings intentionally. The capricious harm done to human beings by polytheistic deities may not be seen to be deliberately evil. Furthermore, this category does not include the beings who harm humanity in the course of pursuing some larger worthy goal, since that will permit human acquiescence even if reluctant. When human beings believe that fear and harm are inevitable or serve a higher end, they will not name such powerful beings with the words we are about to consider, but will probably use gods. No matter how bloodthirsty Kali may be, for example, she is still mother and goddess to her devotees. Rudolf Otto pointed out (in *The Idea of the Holy*) that the experience of any god or numinous being involves fear. Power cannot be power without the possibility of harm as well as benefit. Thus, it would seem that human beings cannot be completely without apprehension before a god, even when the doctrinal assertion of the god's goodness is made.

Non-Hindu religious groups, however, may call Kali, plus many less grisly deities, "devils" in the attempt to explain (away) the Hindu religious tradition in terms of their own theologies. The gods of another religion can be conceived theologically in three basic ways. First, their existence can be completely denied and their myths dismissed as fictions. Second, they can be incorporated into one's theology as precursors or different manifestations of one's own god(s), as different incarnations or avatars, and as angels. Third, they can be understood to be bad spirits or devils.

Like beneficent super-human powers, the malevolent come in varying degrees. At the lowest level of significance and power are those ubiquitous spirits of nature that are at least potentially harmful. "Demon" is almost always used with negative overtones in English although its Greek form *daimon* refers also to helpful extra-human beings. The jinn of Arabic lore and Islamic tradition (English genies) are likewise ambiguous but leaning toward troublesome. Such beings are often blamed for sickness, including what modern people would call mental illness, as well as unaccountable events and losses in daily life.

When the bad spirit tries to affect human beings in their normal consciousness different names and myths are involved. The following set of English terms and conceptions is based on the tradition originating in the Bible and is applied to other religions with varying degrees of accuracy. Devil, despite is more generic usage for all bad spirits, comes from the Greek *diabolos* (whence diabolic, etc.) which means slanderer. It was used by ancient Jews and Christians to translate the Hebrew *satan*, which means adversary or interferer. These words imply social contexts, often something like a law court, in which a satan or devil is the prosecuting attorney. Added to this is the more private and individual role of this figure as a tempter of the human will. These words are used as proper names for a certain evil being or generally for such beings as well as humans who act like them.

A satan or devil does not have to be entirely evil or very powerful but can be both, as the history of the Western religions illustrates. Satan is not used much in the Hebrew Bible except in Job where he is a member of the heavenly court and a skeptic concerning the goodness of Job. In the four centuries preceding the writing of the Christian canon, however, Satan grows in nastiness and power, until, in Christian, then Muslim, theology, he is an arch-enemy to God and man. It is suspicious that this amplification of Satan occurs after the appearance of Zoroastrianism on the scene. In the theology ascribed to Zoroaster the evil being, Ahriman or Angra Mainyu, is very powerful indeed, although probably not thought to be exactly equal to the good god, Ahura Mazdah or Ohrmazd, who eventually will defeat him. There is enough parity here for people to call this "theological dualism." This dualism should not be confused with other two-isms, especially the body-soul dualism of some Greek and most Indian thought.

There are other words, myths, and ideas concerning the bad god or angel in the Western tradition. One is expressed in the name "Lucifer," from the Latin for a bearer of light. There seems to have been an ancient Near Eastern myth about an aerial figure which falls from the sky. It was used by two Hebrew Bible writers to make fun of the pretentious kings of Tyre and Babylon (see Ezekiel 28:12-19 and Isaiah 14:3-21). Going back to the metaphor that these writers used, the Western religious tradition developed a mythology of Satan as Lucifer, an angel associated with light who fell somehow from that status. Many stories are told which describe and account for this fall, including some based on sexual desire, others on pride. In any event, the Lucifer , Satan , Devil figure has had a rich history; it provides a theodicy by blaming much human distress on activities of this fairly powerful angel.

Yet other terms for evil spirits or forces should be noticed. Snakes, serpents, and dragons have been a part of the Western symbolism for the evil force. The New Testament book The Revelation of John, or The Apocalypse, uses a number of names or symbols together in 12:9 and 20:2, "the great dragon, that serpent of old that led the whole world astray, whose name is Satan or the Devil." The serpent referred to here is the creature of the story in Genesis 3. Since he (it) is apparently deprived of legs and feet in Genesis 3:14 we may understand that this serpent is more like a lizard or crocodile, the mythical image being the dragon. As a dragon the evil being has mythical cousins in Tiamat of the Babylonian Creation myth and other life-threatening monsters. Dragons continue to be found in Western iconography as the ocean, hell, and the opponent of St. George. Mouths and fire that consume life seem to be important in dragon imagery. It is curious that dragons in Chinese culture are good, in contrast with their almost totally negative Western connotations.

Now that we have reviewed gods big and little, good and bad, we should take note of one last special category: kings as gods. The Hebrew word *mashiah*, Greek *christos*, English messiah or christ, discussed briefly in chapter 4 and mentioned above in connection with avatars and incarnations, belongs also in this context. These words are based in the ancient Israelite ritual of anointing and thereby consecrating kings as well as prophets and priests in the ceremonies of their accession to these offices. When this term was added to the idea of a future king, perhaps not an ordinary human being, specially sent by God, it became more a term for this chapter than the next (on human beings).

The idea that kings are gods is not unusual, however. The Egyptian pharoah was thought to be Horus and his deceased father Osiris, deities in the Egyptian pantheon. The Japanese emperor was called a manifest *kami*. Although it was already somewhat artificial Hellenistic kings are known to have proclaimed themselves epiphanies of God. The Dalai Lama is thought to be an incarnation of the Bodhisattva Avalokiteshvara. Ancient Israelites seem to have held an interesting compromise notion between human and divine kingship in the idea that the king was an adopted son of God (reading Psalm 2 as a coronation hymn). In these ideas there is a notion of deity, not just a doctrine of a divine mandate or divine right of kings.

We end as we began, with the overlap of words and conceptions for the human and super-human. In the next chapter human beings and their destinies will take center stage.

11 | HUMAN BEINGS

The doctrines concerning human beings in a theology or philosophy are sometimes called its "anthropology," to be distinguished from the use of this word to name an academic discipline concerned with human behavior all over the world. The words used in theologies to identify aspects of human beings and their fate are almost as difficult to nail down as the words for gods. Let us return to the word "spirit." It comes from a word meaning breath. Especially in the plural it expresses intensity of life, vivacity. In the set of words for human beings we should include "soul" and the Latin *anima* with its various formations in English. All of them attempt to name something that makes human beings alive but is often thought to continue somehow after death. The possibilities of meaning for these words range from the essence of mortal life to something immortal and transcendent.

Notice that the idea of life itself is ambiguous in religious language. Sometimes it means something quite close to biological definitions and thus would apply to human beings insofar as they grow, adapt and metabolize. In other contexts, however, religions assert that the deeper essence of a life does not end with physical death or cessation of biological life. This produces strange word combinations with great existential impact in which death and life are not alternatives. Sometimes "afterlife" or "new life" and like combinations point out the difference between ordinary definitions of life and life after death. As life is redefined in these theological contexts so also religions may refer to the dead not as the non-living but as the people who are somehow active but not alive quite the same way we are. The dead are sometimes thought to inhabit corpses and thus look and act like human beings and yet are dead, e.g. zombies.

The meanings of life mentioned so far assume that it is a status or situation one clearly has or does not have. Much other use of the word sees life in a continuum from less to more. One might be literally more dead than alive in this kind of understanding, but still technically alive or alive by other definitions. We may think of this language either as poetic imagery or as proper categorical discrimination, for human life may be something that is more present in people at some times than others. The importance of these conceptual and terminological issues is seen in the discussions about whether fetuses and brain-dead human organisms are alive or are human beings, discussions which affect decisions concerning abortion and euthanasia. In traditional societies the gradual ritual adoption of babies and children into human society also reflects a sense that not all human beings have the same type, amount, or quality of life. Depending on the religion or worldview, therefore, various things may be included in the category of human life, sometimes more and sometimes less than biological definitions include.

One way to distinguish between the various doctrines of human life is to note how long the spirit or soul exists and in what condition. The first possibility is that these words can be used to name an aspect of human life which ceases at physical death. This can be a religious usage in that not all theologies affirm a doctrine of life after death. Second, these words can be used for an aspect of life that does continue after physical death, but not necessarily forever or well. This second idea is close to our usual associations with the word "ghost." I like to describe this kind of idea as left-over life. Something of the vitality of a human being is thought to persist after death, often connected to the corpse and affected by its proper disposal. Ghosts are not thought to be as well-off as live human beings. They may have the power to affect human life a bit but they also need or appreciate signs of respect, food, and other offerings from the living. They may linger in cemeteries and cremation grounds or on the fringes of civilization; they may live deep in the earth or in some other land of the dead. They may be thought to return as ghosts to the world of the living, periodically or on special request. They may be thought able to return by inhabiting corpses, animals, or other physical forms. Also they might somehow re-appear in the birth of new human beings, but without all the implications of reincarnation. Communication with such dead spirits is called "necromancy."

The third major class of possibilities for the meaning of soul or spirit is designated by adding "immortal." Here the aspect of human life that persists beyond death is the best part. It is better off without the body and the limitations of normal human life. It is thought to be imprisoned by a body. It does not need or should not want anything from the living or earthly life itself. It cannot die as the body does, and thus it existed before birth too. An immortal soul concept always involves the idea of incarnation or being put into flesh, because the soul has its own coherent existence and is only temporarily connected with a body. It can also involve reincarnation, which is successive connection with many different bodies. These bodies might be human, animal, anything else on earth, or various unearthly beings both pleasant and unpleasant.

The idea of reincarnation can be found in many theologies but is especially explicit in Indian religious thought and often expressed in Sanskrit terms. The Sanskrit word often translated soul is *atman* which basically means self. This is not usually thought to be the personal self but a deeper essence of life. It transmigrates from life to life or body to body in a process known as *samsara*. For some Hindus the atman is ultimately one with the soul of the universe, called "Brahman," and coming to that recognition is a way of salvation. This set of Hindu terms and ideas is the clearest expression of reincarnation in world religions, but it is known in various transmutations elsewhere. It is sometimes referred to by a word borrowed from the Greek, "metempsychosis," and ancient Greek thinkers toyed with this idea. The Jains in India take this idea to the extreme by assuming that even rocks have souls in the process of transmigration. Buddhists specifically deny the doctrine of the atman but affirm samsara and a kind of reincarnation, difficult as that is to understand at first.

Unlike the Indian tradition, Western religions usually have denied the doctrine of reincarnation despite its appearance in some ancient Greek thought, especially Plato. They have, however, sometimes spoken of the idea of an immortal soul. This idea does not blend too well with other words and doctrines in the Western tradition. Our fourth category of spirit or soul ideas is part of eschatological mythology and revolves around the phrase "resurrection of the dead." In the apocalyptic scenario of Christianity and Islam, those who have died are reconstituted, as it were, and become somehow new psychosomatic (that is, soul and body) wholes. It remains a matter of dispute in these traditions where and how a human being is between death and resurrection. Options include: absolutely non-existent until re-created by God again, asleep, and existing as a soul or ghost in some non-earthly place or in the grave. The doctrine of resurrection differs from the immortal soul doctrine in placing more value in the body (or some new version of it) and in placing greater emphasis on personal identity.

We have had to take note of myths and doctrines concerning other worlds in the course of this discussion. They are more numerous than the terminology for them available in English. Most prominent in English usage are the pair, "heaven" and "hell," for places beyond this world and after death, where human beings receive reward and punishment respectively. To these the term "purgatory" must be added in recognition of the Roman Catholic doctrine of a place of preparation for heaven after death. "Limbo" is another English word that originally named a place of the dead but is generally used for any situation of indeterminacy. It is the place on the border of heaven for people who were not bad and did not deserve hell but were not baptized and thus are barred from heaven. "Paradise" comes from a Persian word meaning garden and has been used to refer to heaven, to an anteroom to heaven, and to the Garden of Eden in Western mythologies.

After these words for different places for the dead, we must resort to other languages to make distinctions. Hades (Greek) and *Sheol* (Hebrew) name roughly similar lands of the dead. They contain both good and bad people, with the Greek tradition being more explicit as to their relative comfort or pleasure. Elysium (the Elysian fields), a pleasant place for the good after death, is in Hades. Both are usually thought to be underground. The western horizon, gravesite of the dying sun, is sometimes the locus of Hades and other realms of the dead. "Hell" has sometimes been used to translate Hades but its usual associations are with places of punishment, alternative to other, more pleasant, afterworlds. Heavens and hells proliferate in Buddhist lore. They are separate places but otherwise like the various levels or areas in Dante's picture of the afterworlds in The Divine Comedy. Each place is suited to the crime or karma of one's previous life. Unlike any Western idea, except purgatory, is the Mahayana Buddhist idea of other worlds where salvation is easier, e.g. the Pure Land.

To return to the conceptions of human beings, so far we have categorized these conceptions according to the length of life involved. Now we can also sort out names and ideas according to human functions and activities. Many human beings have thought that the most remarkable thing about themselves was thought itself. Mind, knowledge, and intellect become crucial, religiously significant words. In such worldviews some or all of thought is understood to be a function of the soul rather than the body.

Many of the words we have discussed in this chapter are based on the assumption of a body-soul dualism of varying degrees of seriousness. The most radical version of this dualism sees all the physical world or matter to be antithetical to the realm of the spiritual, even its enemy and sometime captor. Gnosticism is the classic example of radically dualistic thought in the Western tradition. This term is used by scholars to name a group of religions or philosophical schools in the Hellenistic world. Its name comes from the common emphasis in these systems of thought on knowledge as a saving factor in human life. They also share a depreciation of the physical world. Less radical versions of body-soul dualism still understand the physical to be inferior and of an entirely different nature than the spiritual. Some Greek and most Indian thought follows this line of reasoning.

Some theologies and philosophies divide human beings into three parts making mind or intellect an additional component to body and soul. There can be many souls also, as in ancient Egyptian thought, in which there are at least four. In these cases adjectives must be used in English with "soul," for example "animal soul," or the original languages must be transliterated. It is important to remember that English terminology is not equipped to translate quickly or easily the subtleties of some anthropologies.

Traditional associations with parts of the human body also indicate conceptions of humanity. "Heart" is a good example. It refers commonly today to the seat of emotions but has been thought to be the seat of intellect in older systems. Archaic use of "bowels" for the location of pity and tenderness shows that these emotions were re-located over the centuries. The traditional understanding of the fluids or humors of the body have given us a set of interesting words in English: "sanguine" from the blood and hopeful energy; "melancholic" from the black, sad bile; "phlegmatic" from the sluggish phlegm; and "choleric" from the yellow bile that makes one hot-tempered. Body margins and orifices are also important in mythological biologies.

Psuche and its various combinations in English reflect a traditional and modern difficulty in separating mental and emotional aspects of life, demonstrating perhaps that the separation is more verbal and conceptual than actual. Sometimes words formed using "psych-" refer to any mental phenomena, sometimes especially to the subliminal or unconscious aspects of self or mind, and sometimes to emotions and will more than logical or analytical consciousness. In the specific form "psychic" it has also referred to mental phenomena which are unusual, if not suspicious, like telepathy (feeling or knowing things without the use of the senses), prescience (knowing events before they happen), and mediumship (receiving information and aid from a supernatural agency).

The reason for defining human beings, the soul, or the body in one way or another is rarely idle curiosity and usually not motivated by practical considerations alone. Human life needs definition in a religion usually because life is thought to be incomplete or wrong in some way that warrants human attention. This is the arena of soteriology, the pattern of salvation in religions. Not all religions are equally concerned with salvation, but the pattern which we find explicit in many modern religions is applicable to some ancient traditions, with modification. In its simplest form, a salvation system works like this: It understands something to be seriously wrong in human life. It offers a remedy for this problem and hope for a different, improved situation elsewhere and/or in the future.

Turning to the last stage first, we have discussed heaven as a land of the dead but we see it now as the goal of a soteriological system. Another type of salvation goal is union with the divine or the essence of the world. Still another is the Buddhist nirvana which is sometimes translated extinction, but that does not have the right ring to it. One must understand nirvana as a positive word for a goal worth achieving, despite its conception in terms of what it is not. It is freedom from passion, from bondage to the world, from rebirth, and from all the suffering of life.

It is ironic that a new life after death is the goal of some soteriologies, especially of the Western religions, while the cessation of lives after death is the goal of Indian salvation systems. Of course, much depends on how nice the rebirth is, but beyond that the issue of personality is crucial. The preservation of personal identity is important to anything worth calling salvation for Western people, while others want to transcend that too. Note the discussion of person in Chapter 10, on terminology and understanding of gods.

The words for the problem a soteriology addresses are headed by "sin" in English. Common associations with this word in everyday speech are sex and food, as if the most important sin was mismanagement of the basic appetites. By contrast theological systems have seen such sins as symptoms of a much deeper predicament. The problem of human life according to the Western religions is generally understood to be disobedience. Sin in its strict theological sense, then, is doing what is forbidden or omitting to do what is commanded by one's deity, no matter what it is. In order to conceive of sin in this way one should have a specific set of injunctions derived from the god through revelation. In a little broader sense, sin can be thought to be transgression of general principles. It then becomes possible to postulate sinfulness in light of a natural theology; that is, one should know through reason and conscience the general rules which the god demands. In a yet broader sense, however, sin can be disengaged from revelation entirely, referring to things thought to be inherently bad without any reference to a god and obedience.

There are other words and categories for the soteriological problem. It can be understood intellectually, as a problem of ignorance (*avidya* in Sanskrit). It can be described as desire or longing, e.g. for fulfillment. It can be seen in dramatic ways such as being imprisoned, trapped, or lost and wandering. It can be understood as a lost integrity or a need to transcend the limitations of humanity. It can be focused on death as the chief and final insult to life, or on rebirth into another existence doomed to suffering and another death. In the Buddhist analysis, the root problem is suffering caused by desire. All these perspectives are usually expressed individually but can be understood communally. When a soteriological pattern is applied to whole societies the problem can be political or military as in the conquest by an enemy power and enslavement, or it can be the diminution of the food supply. Usually, however, the soteriological pattern is more explicit in individual applications.

Once the problem is identified, many means of rectifying it may be recommended. The techniques for gaining salvation form a large area of religious thought and activity. Since we started the analysis of soteriology by considering sin as disobedience, the first means of salvation we should take note of is obedience, abiding by all the injunctions of the deity. These laws include things which could be divided between the categories of ritual and morality, but the distinction is not necessarily made. It can be as sinful to eat pork and blaspheme as it is to murder or commit adultery, so obedience will take ritual and/or moral forms. Just returning to obedience from disobedience may not be enough, however, in which case rituals to erase and compensate for disobedience may be prescribed, and special, extra acts may be expected.

Rites and good deeds might also be included among the techniques of salvation from soteriological problems other than disobedience. However, ignorance more immediately calls for meditation and education. Other problems might demand yogic discipline, asceticism, or other modification of life. These possibilities are often blended together in religious practice no matter what the soteriological problem. The language of religiously significant human acts will be covered in the next chapters.

Many kinds of soteriological activity also blend with recourse to a "savior." This is a term for the kind of super-natural figure who helps human beings in the salvation process. The help can vary in degree from a little to everything. Amida Buddha helps by making sure that his devotees are reborn in his Pure Land. There they will have to do the rest of their salvation on their own, but it is much easier there than here. Some people think that the savior figure helps by erasing old sins or deficits but then requires certain responses or acts in this life or in another. Most savior figures are thought to be able or willing to help only if some act of mind or body, e.g. an act of faith, is performed by the human being in need of salvation, but this act may be minimal.

A special kind of theological issue occurs in a number of theologies when the savior does everything including the minimal response. Gratefulness is the expectable appropriate response to the beneficial aid of the savior, but it seems to go overboard in those theologies where even the trust one puts in a savior is said to come from the savior. As an expression of one's personal debt to the savior, statements of complete helplessness and gratitude are understandable, but theological problems arise when this conception becomes part of a theological system. The word "predestination" names the doctrine that all human beings who are saved have been selected by the savior before their births to be saved and they do nothing except live out that destiny. If every human being is so selected, the savior's goodness is preserved, but most soteriologies assume that some people are not saved.

These theologies are forced into a dilemma not unlike the problem of theodicy. Double predestination is the idea that the damned are predestined to their fate as well as the saved to theirs. Even though they want to maintain the doctrine of a good savior god, these theologies posit a god who does not select certain people for salvation and thus predestines them to failure and punishment. That seems unjust.

The human side of the dilemma raises the question of free will. For soteriologies the central issue is the human role in salvation. It may or may not be linked to a notion of the predetermination of all of life. The latter idea evokes words like "fate," "fortune," "luck," as conscious and/or immutable prescriptions for life. These can be personified and deified (Lady Luck, The Fates, etc.). Strict philosophical notions of determinism are formulated in terms of impersonal cause and effect. Determinisms come in harder or softer versions, depending on the degree to which an individual is thought to be able to change the course of events.

In this chapter we have moved from language that defines human beings according to what they are, to language concerning what they do, specifically in connection with gaining salvation. Now we should reflect on human activity even more directly and that demands a new chapter.

12 | MORAL ACTIVITY

We have noted in connection with sin and its rectification that religious laws may command ritual as well as moral acts. This indicates that the realm of religiously significant acts is larger than either category taken alone. The total relevant category we must analyze is the whole gamut of religiously prescribed or deliberate human acts. Religious traditions do not necessarily make this division between the moral and the ritual. Nevertheless, this chapter will focus on the moral side of the whole area of religious activity, and the next chapter will focus on the ritual.

Morality as religious activity ranges from matters of almost complete indifference to those which are punished by death. It includes minor formalities as well as heroic self-sacrifice. Therefore, one way of organizing the words for religiously significant acts is along a continuum of evaluations from important to trivial. Note well, however, that the evaluations used in the following paragraphs are those of the modern student of religions and not necessarily those of people within religious traditions. Again let us note, the latter often take matters of ritual more seriously than is appropriate from the characteristically modern point of view.

The most serious and inclusive of the evaluative words for human activity in modern usage is "moral." Acts and people are called moral when they are right, proper, ideal, and important. The word is sometimes used loosely along with "ethical" as if they were synonymous, but the latter emphasizes the social dimension and moral tends to be used of an individual's sense of right and wrong. "Ethos," transliterated directly from the Greek, means character, especially of a group of people, and "ethnic" is applied to the characteristics which make cultural units distinguishable. Both moral and ethical can be used descriptively or normatively: A moral question is one that concerns what is right and wrong without indicating whether the question is good or bad, but a moral person or act is a good person or act.

In the study of morals or ethics a contrast exists between descriptive and normative approaches. The latter seeks to establish what really is right and wrong, to discover basic laws for human conduct or, failing these, some directives and values. That task is very important in any society and for any reflective individual. The descriptive task, however, is simply to find out what the moral practices, principles, and motivations are in any society or religious tradition. One strives in this context not to prescribe but to understand without prejudice. Such understanding might even help in subsequent normative evaluation, but the two tasks must be kept distinct. Descriptive analysis is faulty and cannot help the normative task if it is skewed by the normative position of the investigator. Cannibalism can be a good test of the descriptive mode. It is unlikely to be commended by most people, and yet the descriptive study of ethics seeks to discover its rationality and goodness in certain cultures. Comparative religious ethics is a growing field of study based on this descriptive program.

Both morality and ethics are more inclusive and have higher authority, in the modern religions at least, than law. "Law" can be used in connection with natural processes and prevailing non-human practice, for example, law of gravity or law of the jungle. Human law, however, is based on the notion of socially enforced rules of conduct. Civil law is usually limited to observable behavior and enforceable regulations in contrast with morality which can also apply to thoughts and private acts. When civil law deals with intentions
and motives it does so only in connection with acts, although it

is formulated sometimes to cover private acts when some public effect is anticipated.

Religious laws are different from civil law in a number of ways, one of which is the inclusion of private thoughts and acts, since the ultimate enforcer of the laws knows the heart, whether that enforcer is God or oneself. Some religions are more concerned with law than others, for example, Judaism's most revered religious texts are called torah, which is translated "law." Religious traditions concentrate on law when the religion and the state are not distinguished and/or when obedience to a god or a natural moral law is important. Other religions, however, relegate matters of social morality to a subsidiary level, perhaps preparatory to or assumed within the larger framework of a salvation process.

Civil law can cover matters which are not always thought to be morally important. The patterns of the economy, the regulation of vehicular traffic, the testing of products for factors other than health and safety, and many other functions of government may or may not be thought to have ethical ramifications. Law, understood as the body of rules of behavior for a government, can be different from the set of rules appropriate to individual persons, a prominent example of which is the act of killing another human being. Note the acceptance of capital punishment and warfare as acts of government within the same cultures which ban individual acts of killing. What is prohibited to individuals in such situations needs a separate word, murder. The prohibition in these cases is against killing which is unauthorized by the rest of the society, the moral or legal system, and God. Complete prohibition of killing is commonly called "pacifism" or is expressed more radically in the Sanskrit word popularized by Gandhi: *ahimsa*, non-injury.

"Custom" and "etiquette" are words for a definitely lower level of concern regarding human activity. We recognize that social groups and large cultural units share certain notions as to how things should be done but they do not always elevate them to the status of law, let alone the force of moral principles. It may be inelegant to eat using fingers or the wrong implement; it may be impolite and therefore potentially dangerous not to bow, salute, or kowtow before authority figures. Such acts are usually classified as customs or matters of etiquette in contemporary usage. The assumption is that they do not have the importance of law and morality, but are still prescribed, expected behavior patterns, and moral fervor can be attached to them on occasion.

If English speakers say that some practice is a matter of "convention" they are indicating that they understand it to be fairly unimportant, a matter of consent and agreement for practical reasons. Conventional practices concerning where to walk in relationship to others, which gender is expected to perform what acts (like opening doors), and many similar matters of everyday life vary from culture to culture and are subject to change within each culture. The efficiency of daily activity is at stake but also the relationship of people to each other. Because of the personal aspect, these matters can take on unexpected importance.

One of the big differences between traditional and modern cultures is the application of moral sentiment to language and ceremony. "Profanity" and "blasphemy" are terms for morally culpable misuse of sacred words. Modern mentality, by contrast, tends to give moral weight to word usage only insofar as it has harmful psychological effects or is deceiving. Contemporary English speakers, therefore, usually put the proprieties of communication in the realm of etiquette. Traditional religion, however, often holds that words can have real effects in the natural and social worlds. Magical formulas, *mantras*, curses, and blessings really change things, not just minds. Contrary to the modern proverb, names can hurt as much as sticks and stones, and not only emotionally. Similarly, ritual acts are not merely symbolic, as modern people might say, but are means by which one can transform both people and the natural world. Therefore, what the modern student calls "custom," "convention," "etiquette," or "ritual" may be quite different in character and importance to the traditional religious person. Contemporary societies are not consistently modern, of course, since laws and moral outrage are occasionally applied to what is considered misuse of national flags and other prominent symbols.

A lot of traditional religious moral language revolves around words like "purity" rather than "goodness." Understanding many moral systems involves a shift of attention for modern analysts from acts and behavior back to the being or essential nature of the person who acts or of the things involved in human acts. Many acts are wrong in traditional moralities because in doing that act a person or a physical thing becomes impure, polluted, unclean, or something which it is not supposed to be. The terminology of purity is often linked with words for dirt and cleanliness, which are its chief area of metaphor or symbolic expression. The interpenetration of ritual and morality is very extensive in this language, and it becomes even more confused when linked with modern notions of hygiene. "Impurity" can mean any or all of the following: ritual impropriety, moral transgression, physical pollution, health-threatening practices, and the unnatural.

Modern people often misread ancient purity language because they think of it in terms of modern moral categories, and in medical and chemical contexts. Neither frame of reference is dominant in ancient texts although a theologian may argue that they are latent or intended by God. Clearly, however, ancient texts declare certain foods, animals, diseases, and bodily conditions unclean, and prohibit or regulate them in order to protect society. These things are deemed wrong because they do not fit in the prevailing conceptions of order and propriety, because they are dangerous, and because God wants society to be properly ordered and safe.

One example which is regularly misunderstood are the declarations and regulations of impurity connected with menstruation. These do not declare women periodically unclean in the characteristically modern moral or medical senses of the term, but they indicate the value and power of blood. Since blood is often thought to be the essence of life itself, it may be prohibited as food, used as a powerful ritual element, and feared when it is outside its proper, guarded places. Bleeding indicates power out of control, so special precautions and restrictions are required. Things that are unclean and impure are dangerous.

More recent Puritans, however, are not in this thought-world but have applied purity language to moral, social interaction. The word "Puritan" originally referred to a program for purifying the Christian church in England, but it turned out to be suited also to the kind of moral theology espoused by the purifying reformers. They preached a moral sensitivity and a suspicion of human pleasure which became known beyond their immediate circle as the puritan spirit. This leads directly to the contemporary connotations of pure which revolve around notions of chastity, innocence, and simplicity. In this instance as in many others the same words are used for ritual as for moral value, but the latter category, being more important in modern thought, overshadows the former. Where the ritual language is not associated with morality, however, modern people have trouble understanding the sense of importance that traditional peoples placed on ritual propriety. We will take up the language of ritual again a little later.

We have placed many words for human activity in a continuum from the most inclusive and serious to the least important. Another continuum we can use is the degree of abstraction or generality. "Principles" is usually used for the most abstract notions of right and wrong, but principles have varying degrees of generality or universality themselves. At the other extreme are very specific injunctions or commands with specific application. For example, moral principles might enjoin, in descending generality, respect for all people, respect for people in your nation or race, respect for those people from whom one has received benefit, and respect for certain kinds of people considered to be greater than you in value or prestige. At the most specific level, "Honor your father and mother," identifies two people only. Moral discussion regularly expands the specific by analogy and applies the generic to specific cases.

A kind of specificity is also involved in another discrimination within the realm of moral discourse. Sometimes moral laws are expressed in terse absolute or apodictic law, with no ifs or buts. This is often also personal, as in "You shall not steal." Much ancient and most modern law, however, is expressed in conditional or casuistic form, postulating a situation and the procedure for settling it, for example, "If a burglar is caught in the act and fatally injured, it is not murder, unless he breaks in after sunrise." (based on Exodus 22: 2-4) "Casuistry" has gotten a bad name as a method of analyzing moral situations because it is thought to be a way of avoiding the real issues or arguing speciously.

Casuistry illustrates the tension between various forms of expression or degrees of abstraction in moral and legal analysis. Another example is the term "situation ethics" which indicates that the good can be discovered only in particular situations as compared to general prescriptions. It would seem that some people are informed and motivated more by specific demands than general principles, and are suspicious of those who place greater weight on the more abstract, conditional forms of moral direction, and vice versa.

Philosophical theorizing regarding morality is irrelevant to theologies which base their notions of right and wrong solely on ancient texts and practices. In these theological systems the only study of morality is the study of the canonical sources, with application by extrapolation and analogy from them. Some religious as well as secular ethical systems, however, attempt to establish reasons why certain kinds of acts are good or better than others. If one's god is thought to have given human beings more discretion and choice in determining how to apply general principles of religion, one can use methods of philosophical analysis in a religious way. Given the possibility of this application it is appropriate here to consider some of the terminology of philosophical moral analysis.

Many thinkers see morality arising out of a sense of obligation and responsibility. The word "deontological" (necessity, duty) is given to this approach, especially as it is compared to "utilitarianism" (utility), the moral analysis based on the greatest good for the greatest number of people. Duty and responsibility are the key words for deontological ethics. It is rooted in considerations of the goodness of an action in itself rather than by analysis of its consequences. In India a similar notion is called *dharma*, the law of what people are supposed to do. It is more difficult to determine what one should do according to the utilitarian approach, because one must go beyond the action itself to a consideration of its results in the given situation. A simple example: As a duty taken alone it is good to speak the truth, but the utilitarian approach may argue that some lies produce more good in the short and long run while truthfulness might be cruel and harmful in certain circumstances.

We have just noted the Sanskrit word dharma. It is one of a set of Indian words which have become a part of English and its language of morality. It is a difficult word with an extensive history in Indian religions. One common meaning is duty but another is teaching, a meaning that is prominent in Buddhism. Dharma is expanded in Buddhist philosophy to mean the aspects of phenomenal reality. All these meanings may be seen to be applications of its root idea, the established order.

Another example of the Sanskrit words which have entered English is "karma." Each person according to Hindu belief has a certain *karman* which is the quality of one's life or the relative place one has attained in the process of ultimate transformation. If one's karma is relatively poor it produces pain in this life and a less fortunate rebirth, but a good karmic state leads to higher quality life now, better reincarnation, and eventually *moksha*, release, or nirvana, extinction. Karma basically means actions, not as ephemeral events but as elements in a chain of cause and effect. The ways of salvation adjust or redirect this chain but it continues inexorably throughout one's entire existence, through eons. All bad actions are eventually punished and all good rewarded; one can blame only oneself (in previous lives as well as this one) for the quality of present existence.

"Conscience" is an interesting word in the language of morality. It has philosophical background but much religious application. It names a supposed intuition or moral faculty in each person which motivates one to do the good and even determine what the good is. As a way of emphasizing the role of individual decision in moral matters, the term is clear. As a source of moral direction, however, it is problematic, because one is not sure from most uses of the word just what causes or directs conscience.

The words used for specific moral injunctions are extensive and can be problematic. A few outstanding examples deserve some attention. The Arabic word jihad has become widely used by English speakers recently and for most of them it simply means holy war waged by Muslims against those they understand to be non-Muslims opposed to Islam. The objects of jihad can include people who think of themselves as Muslims, but are not really such in the eyes of the wagers of jihad. As with many emotionally charged terms, some people are worried that others may not understand the word correctly, so a program of lexical education is being undertaken in defense of an Islam which is misrepresented in this belligerent meaning. Some Muslims and Islamicists point out that the Arabic word refers to all efforts made to strengthen Islam, especially the interior disciplines of each pious Muslim. In this larger framework, warfare is only an extreme possibility of an ongoing program of obedience and submission to God. Language use and its background prejudices are not easily adjusted, however. Only as the public image of Islam among English speakers shifts in the direction of greater appreciation of its beneficent intentions, will "jihad" be expanded or abandoned.

The language of sexual immorality is sometimes confusing. "Incest" names those prohibitions against marriage or sexual intercourse with related persons. The problems occur in determining what relationships are so prohibited. "Exogamy" is the more technical term for the rules excluding some otherwise potential marriage partners, but they are based on kinship conceptions that are not necessarily apparent to all cultures. Another kind of restriction works in the opposite direction. "Endogamy" prohibits marriage outside a defined group. "Adultery" is also ambiguous. It may be extended to refer to all sexual activity outside of marriage, but its more restricted meaning is voluntary sexual intercourse of a married person with another person and thus does not apply to intercourse involving only unmarried people.

Finally, a discussion of morality should take note of its opposite. "Immoral" designates that which is specifically opposed to the moral. "Amoral," like "nonmoral," however, indicates something which is outside the realm of morality. When a person is called amoral a negative tone is connoted under the assumption that people should always be moral even if some few acts are outside the arena of morality. "License" has two meanings: it names that which is permitted by special arrangement under law, but also the lack of lawfulness. "Licentious" almost always has the negative sense of lawlessness where law should apply, especially in sexual matters.

The most inclusive meaning of "evil" can be found in the contrast between what we do not like and what we find either indifferent or beneficial. Many doctrines or theories concerning the origin or nature of evil have been proposed and what constitutes evil varies widely. There are natural evils like earthquakes and social evils like war; people as well as acts and sometimes things are called evil. All these are evil because some human beings have made judgments concerning what they prefer or value. That which impedes or destroys those valued things goes into a common category and is loaded with opprobrium.

13 | RITUAL ACTIVITY

Turning our attention directly to matters of ritual, let us begin at the beginning, the word "rite" itself, with its compounds. Ritual is recognized in animal and human behavior when acts which might possibly be utilitarian are either condensed or exaggerated, and repeated unnecessarily. The same kinds of factors describe a kind of human behavior which is irrational and obsessive, called compulsions. What differentiates religious ritual from animal behavior and compulsive human behavior is the assumption that it is voluntary. Religious rituals may come to be quite automatic or habitual in human life, but other words and analyses will be used when there is a sense that the behavior is predominantly determined by psychological, physical, or instinctual demands.

While rituals certainly serve some purpose, the telltale sign of this category is the suppression or lack of any kind of usefulness beyond the rite itself. It is really just happy coincidence if traditional rites serve some practical purpose, and they are as likely to be inefficient or harmful from a pragmatic point of view. For example, the ritual of washing hands before meals was discovered to be hygienic millennia after it was instituted, but blood-spilling and mutilation rites such as subincision and clitorectomy are probably detrimental physically. I am recommending a "rite for rite's sake" approach to understanding ritual.

If rites are not performed in order to achieve practical ends, why are they performed at all? The intrinsic purpose of ritual is to be found in understanding it in terms of expressive perfor-mance, and as a kind of language. The word "language" has been discussed in chapter 7 where its applicability to the arts was mentioned. Ritual may be understood as an art and as an artistic language or blend of languages. It is especially kin to theater or drama because it includes the same combination of various means of expression: words, music, gesture, dance, and visual arts (as they are involved in set and costume design).

However, "art" is a difficult word to use in connection with analysis of ritual because it has associations which do not fit this context. Art has long meant skill and learning, thus implying both professionalism and gracefulness. This runs counter to the emphasis in rite on the thing done as compared to the style or finesse with which it is done. Works of art used in rituals (or taken to be manifestations of holiness) are not necessarily beau-tiful from a purely artistic point of view. In fact, while it might be thought desirable for rituals to be performed in a beautiful man-ner, they are considered to be valid and successful religiously even when they are clumsy or inelegant. Some religious groups appreciate the artistic enhancement of their rituals, but others have sensed that too much attention can be given to the artistic aspects of ritual and have reduced them as much as possible, for example by prohibiting pictorial arts or instrument music in their rites and ritual buildings.

If one uses art as a name for the non-verbal expressive lan-guages, rather than for the skill or craft with which they may be used, it may point to useful distinctions in the dynamics of ritual. Both believers and students of religion have a choice in how they understand the role of the languages of art in religious set-tings. For some people, works of art and rituals are merely decorations or pedagogical devices for communicating the im-portant stories and ideas concerning life and religion. For other people, however, they are the very stuff of such ideas. Opinions vary between saying that the realm of non-verbal communication illustrates and embroiders the otherwise known, to the difficult position that what art and rite say cannot be said in any other way, or at least as well.

In the area of religious graphic arts this contrast may be seen in the use of two words built on the word "icon," meaning representation, and used especially for the pictures used in Eastern Orthodox Christian churches. One of these words, "iconography," is fairly common and names the study of the non-verbal signals which identify persons and scenes in religious art, signals which are easily translated into ordinary words. Thus, if one sees a picture of a man crucified upside down or an inverted Christian cross, it most probably pictures or refers to St. Peter. The rarer word, "iconology," is based on a perception that the meaning of much symbolism really lies in the non-verbal form, for which the verbal name is a pale reflection at best. The cross, the reversal of usual human uprightness, and much else in a picture of St. Peter have extensive and essentially visual meanings and associations which verbal analysis struggles to convey. Both iconography and iconology attempt to interpret the symbols of religious art but with different degrees of belief in their importance, necessity, or primacy.

Closely related to this question of the meaning and role of art is the controversy concerning the meaning of idol and idolatry. If one assumes that pictures or statues merely refer to hidden powers and realities, then they are or should be dispensable, somewhat the way iconographic symbols can be replaced by words. From this point of view, works of art which are the focus of ritual acts and worship are just visual aids. Some interpretations of the use of art in worship go to the other extreme, however, and suppose that idols are the actual objects of religious veneration. This is the classic position or apprehension of those who oppose using works of art as objects of ritual attention. These people sometimes become iconoclasts, or image breakers. In between these poles of interpretation lies the position parallel to that of iconology. From this perspective a work of religious art can be deeply meaningful and therefore stand for the reality not otherwise known, without that reality being completely identified with it. There may be real idolaters in the world, but they must be among the more simple-minded of religious folk. Many others who use religious art ritually assume that they are dealing with an expression or manifestation of the transcendent more than a wooden or metal deity, whatever that could mean.

This discussion brings us to the concept of sacrament in Christianity, with possible extension to other religions. Sometimes "sacrament" is used very loosely to mean any rite, but it has more specific application in Christian liturgics (the study of ritual or liturgy). There it is restricted to certain rites in which there is believed to be a physical embodiment of a blessing or presence. This idea is most apparent in the doctrines concerning the bread and wine in the Mass (or Holy Communion or Eucharist), which are understood to be the bearers, in some way, of the body or presence of Jesus. Much discussion has revolved around how that is to be understood. Some Christians speak of a physical presence others of symbolic presence, but there is general agreement on the special attention given to the ritual elements. Thus the word sacrament ranges in meaning, like symbol and art, from superficial and replaceable to essential and unique. In all these words, the variety in meanings is due to different estimations of the role of words, acts, and things in communication, expression, and embodiment of transcendent reality.

The phenomenon of rite implies some measure of formality or stylization of human behavior. There have been people who have tried to minimize this sense of prescription, coordination, and thus imposition upon human freedom of action. However, it is very hard to escape something like ritual whenever many people try to do something together. The Quaker meeting with its insistence that nothing be prescribed except the silence from which some statement or act can emerge, or the attempt to be completely spontaneous in a Holiness church, for another example, merely demonstrate that ritual prescription may be minimal but never completely absent. These assemblies and others like them fall into a pattern of action, intended or not, and this prevails unless one works very hard to be innovative.

Ritual, like other words for means of expression and communication, can be used to name kinds of behavior which are secular rather than specifically religious, although that is the oldest reference of the word. Rite names a kind of vehicle and thus does not presume a specific kind of content, character, or intention. As formal activities, however, rituals tend to give a semi-religious aura to any secular institutions with which they are connected. When nations observe patriotic rituals a sense of religious-like dignity is almost inevitable. With modern self-consciousness about the power of rituals in religious contexts, leaders in a society institute rituals in order to promote certain attitudes, for example pledging allegiance to a nation's flag in order to advance political unity. Etiquette and the ceremonies of inter-personal politeness and decorum are not necessarily religious and yet they also can be deeply felt, as we have noted when discussing them in the last chapter in association with moral sentiment.

Some words related to ritual indicate the dual role of act and word in rites. "Rubric" refers to a direction for what to do in a ritual and is derived from the medieval practice of writing or printing such words in red to differentiate them from the words which are recited or chanted. "Ceremony" or "ceremonial" deals with the acts of a ritual. "Liturgy," however, is used for both the acts and words of a rite. Music is optional in ritual but the recitation of prescribed words often approaches something one might want to call music, especially in the patterned tonal recitation known as chant. Ritual almost always involves special paraphernalia, furniture, and clothing, but the terminology for these things is either common or so specialized that we shall not review them given the general nature of this book.

Other words associated with ritual move us beyond the public, communal side of ritual with which the terminology reviewed so far is primarily concerned. "Worship" is a more inclusive word, generally assumed to cover most rituals, plus acts not usually called rites. Worship more specifically names the inner sentiment of a person who is performing certain rituals in a certain way. Not all rites presume worship nor is all worship expressed in ritual form, according to this personal, interior understanding of the word. Worship is closely associated with praise, devotion, reverence, and the like, all of which imply that these emotions are interpersonal. Therefore, only rituals which are directed toward other people or personal gods have the character of worship. Other kinds of rites, which are not acts of devotion to a god, might be called magic by those who favor a person-oriented theology, but they are legitimate parts of many religious systems nevertheless. Phenomena called worship, however, can be very private and spontaneous, involving little bodily activity, and thus outside the standard meaning of rite.

Indian religions have a name for worship in *puja*. This kind of religious activity is similar or identical to acts of hospitality and gestures of respect for a distinguished person. It can, of course, be ritualized, that is, it can be prescribed and formalized, and it can be performed pro forma, without the appropriate emotions of worship. In any event *puja* gives expression to devotion to the deity through the same acts of kindness and politeness one would show to one's human superiors and loved ones. This includes offerings of services (e.g. washing), food, and words of praise and delight.

It is instructive also to examine the various meanings of the word "sacrifice." In many ancient cultures vegetable products, animals, and human beings are sacrificed with ritual elaboration and intention. One way that sacrificers might understand their rituals include the notion of repeating the basic sacrifice on which the whole world is based. This is thought to be necessary to the continuation of life and to repair physical or moral failures. It is quite a different thing, perhaps as old, older, or a later development, to understand such sacrifices as offerings to gods. In this second approach sacrifices become part of the mentality of worship, as acts of devotion to personal deities. Typically in the history of religions, the act of sacrifice itself is eventually abandoned and the word reinterpreted as the interpersonal, devotional implications are recognized. Then the gods, it is said, do not really need or want bloody or burnt sacrifices, but are pleased instead with the sacrifice of a contrite or loving heart, or acts of self-sacrifice, moral or ascetic.

One specialized word for a kind of sacrifice, "holocaust," has taken on new meanings in the twentieth century. The ancient Hebrew rules for sacrificing animals distinguished between rites in which the whole victim was burnt and those in which the victim was shared by God, the priest, and the person offering the sacrifice. By the way, the latter phenomenon indicates the idea of companionship (eating together) or communion that also is associated with sacrifices. It is the whole victim sacrifice, however, which was called "holocaust" in Greek, then Latin and English. Since the Second World War it has been applied to the killing of millions of Jewish people by the Nazi regime in Germany, thus interpreting their deaths as sacrifices.

Some other words are used for ritual acts as well as non-ritual worship. "Prayer" can refer to private thoughts or words which are not prescribed and therefore not in the category of rite, but when they are vocalized by one person in the presence of others they enter a ritual context. As ritual, this is sometimes called *ex corde* prayer, or prayer from the heart, but for the listeners it is not necessarily distinguishable from prescribed, pre-written prayer except in their notion of how it is generated. Understood ritually prayers are part of the text of a ritual, distinguished from other texts in being addressed to a deity or person of authority. Prayers excerpted from rituals or written for private use can be used by individuals alone, thus indicating another overlap of ritual and worship.

Recognizing that worship refers more to inner attitudes than outer actions raises the problem of the relationship of these two dimensions. If we focus on the kind of act in defining ritual terms, as well we should, the reason for the act will vary. But if we begin our inquiry with the reasons why people do rites, we discover many possible acts which may follow. One of the subtlest problems of religious life, as T. S. Eliot remarked in *Murder in the Cathedral*, is "to do the right thing for the wrong reason." This is true of moral acts, but even more of ritual acts since the latter are symbols and therefore are right only to the extent that they refer to or represent the appropriate realities. One instance of what can be called wrong in ritual matters is to continue to perform a rite when its reason has been forgotten or changed. This makes "magic" out of ritual according to some theories concerning the relationship of these categories (see chapter 3). It can also lead to ritualism in the negative sense, namely, the practice of rites in a mechanical, insincere manner with little or no regard for the significance or importance of words or acts. The dissociation of rite from intention, taken one step further, to the supposition that quite different and unworthy motives lie behind ritual activity, is expressed in the word "hypocrisy," from the Greek meaning to act a role in a play.

"Piety" and "religiosity" are words that can refer to the whole area of one's prescribed or habitual religious behavior. They may be thought to include conscious moral acts but also rituals and personal practices. A pietist is one who cultivates religious emotion with the use of rites and acts of private worship. We discussed that word in chapter seven, on religious experience. The term has been especially used of a movement in seventeenth century German Protestantism. To be pious is to be conspicuously involved in specifically religious activity.

Some religious activities do not seem to qualify either as worship or ritual. Various forms of meditation, yogic discipline, and the like are not directed to another being nor necessarily performed communally. "Discipline" is one of the few regularly-used English words we have for this kind of activity. We are attempting to name activities which people perform for religious self-improvement, attainment of a higher status or integrity. They can be practiced in groups
and thus have semi-ritual character, but are essentially

individual acts, successful only if they help each practitioner to attain some new powers. Some of these activities or disciplines are not especially arduous or painful but the ones that are fall into the category of asceticism. Ascetic acts may be used in a ritual context, especially as preparation for rites, or as ritual compensation or punishment for sin ("penance"). In other contexts, however, asceticism is part of a program for changing oneself into a different, better being.

Asceticism names actions and deliberate omission of actions either of which normally produce discomfort or pain. The reason given for ascetic acts may not be the production of pain, but practices which are not at least uncomfortable some of the time are not included in the category. Eating ice cream will not qualify as an ascetic act unless it is deliberately done to surfeit or in some other unpleasant way. There is in its etymology and its religious use a sense of athleticism about asceticism. Disciplines of the body oriented towards achievement of higher status or success in some endeavor are similar whether status and success are understood in transcendent terms or not. One therefore affirms and perhaps enjoys such painful discipline, no matter how unpleasant it would be to others, if it is understood to lead to worthwhile goals.

Fasting is a common form of asceticism; it can be confusing insofar as it refers to many kinds of food restriction. Muslim fasting during Ramadan is complete, even excluding water, from sunrise to sunset. By contrast, traditional Christian Lenten fasting prevails day and night for many days but excludes only certain kinds of foods. "Celibacy" is a word for another ascetic act, again one of omission, namely not getting married. The person who happens not to be married but has made no vow or commitment to remain single, like the person who skips a meal through lack of hunger or time, is not thought to be celibate or ascetic. Other forms of asceticism are deliberate acts rather than deprivations. Flagellation, wearing uncomfortable or insufficient clothing, sitting amongst fires under a hot sun, and living on top of a pillar are some historical examples.

The non-ascetic religious disciplines include some which are physical and some mental. The former include yoga, as the practice of maintaining certain physical postures and breath-control. "Yoga" in this sense is a part of the classic yoga system in Hinduism, associated with Patanjali's *Yoga Sutras*. Yoga also refers to any one of a number of Hindu religious paths of which the classic yoga is only one, including devotional or worship-oriented bhakti which is quite different from Patanjali's yoga in doctrine and practice. Classical yoga, along with the sitting meditation of some schools of Buddhism, illustrate the mixture of such physical practices with mental practices and goals. For these matters we have few words in English and must often resort to other languages.

"Meditation" is the overworked word used for many of these Eastern practices as well as somewhat different ones in Western religions. The kind of meditation which is characteristic of Western religions could be called "discursive" in that it regularly consists of reading inspirational texts and thinking about a pious theme. Characteristically Eastern meditation is geared to stopping the flow of thoughts and achieving a state of mind in which there is only one object of thought or none at all. *Dhyana* in Sanskrit, *chan* in Chinese, and *zen* in Japanese, refers to the whole set of practices of this sort and to their goal, a calm, clear, state of mental concentration. *Samadhi* is used for a state yet beyond the highest type of dhyana which is obviously hard to put into words but which is described by phrases like pure consciousness.

We have strayed a bit from the field of ritual in the more precise sense. There is much more language concerning it which warrants our attention. Some special terms are associated with the occasions of ritual activity. Many kinds of rites are performed at crucial transition points in the life-course of individuals, communities, and nature. The last are called "seasonal rites" and they celebrate agricultural, astronomical, and calendrical transitions.

The special moments in the lifetime of an individual are often called "rites of passage" and ritually mark such events as birth, puberty, marriage, and death. Scholars have taken special notice of the structure of these rites as "initiations." Fairly obviously, the move from one status to another involves leaving the former (often symbolized as a death), moving through a transitional period, and entering the new status, for which the major symbol is rebirth. The period in between is called liminal from the Latin for threshold, and is especially interesting for its time-out role in regard to normal life.

Communities of various sorts and sizes are involved in the celebration of individual and natural transitions, but social implications and dynamics are especially apparent in certain rites. For example, the inaugurations, ordinations, and professions which mark the beginning of a person's special role in society validate and help people remember that role. This is especially necessary if the role involves authority and public obedience. These rites start to shift our attention toward the subject of the next chapter, but a few matters may be more appropriately addressed in this one.

"Cult" is a word which is used both for ritual and for a type of religious community. As a word for a set of ritual practices it is almost identical in usage to rite. As a word for a group of people it emphasizes the group's relatively small numbers and unpopularity. Something of the meaning of occult may affect the use of cult because they look and sound so similar. "Occult" primarily names the sense of mystery and secrecy which some groups deliberately cultivate in connection with their rites. Since ritual language is a symbol system, no matter how much it is based in natural gestures, it always demands some education. Outsiders to the ritual group (the exoteric perspective) cannot be expected to understand ritual activity the way insiders (esoteric) do, no matter how open or public the rites. This inevitable privacy of the symbol-using group is reinforced when the members of the group deliberately exclude outsiders and refuse to explain their practices. The "mystery religions" of the Roman Empire and various secret societies have made exclusion from their rites a major factor of their identity. This affects their public image (often negatively) and is (positively) an attractive feature in recruitment and important in the group's social cohesion.

14 | SOCIAL PATTERNS

The words concerning social patterns which demand our attention here can be divided into two types. First there are those involving the leadership of groups and special roles played by individuals. Second are those for the various kinds of groups themselves. It will be profitable to consider the words for types of groups interspersed with the relevant words for various kinds of roles.

The word "cult" links the last chapter's focus on ritual with the social focus of this chapter, and indicates that a word with neutral application in one domain can be negative in another. "The cult of Mary" merely names the rites of devotion to her, but "the Manson cult" brings up images of a secret, evil club. The change in meaning occurs as one shifts from things people do, to the people doing them, and from devotion to a god, to allegiance to a human leader. Cult as a kind of group is often used loosely to refer to any group of which the writer or speaker disapproves. Used more carefully and less judgmentally the cult as a social structure is distinguished from other types of religious groups by its relatively small size and its domination by one person.

The leader of a cult must have something we call "charisma." However, charisma is really not just what one person has but what happens between such a person and others. The personalities and interactions of leaders and followers come together in certain situations to create powerful bonds. In intense cases the control of the followers by a charismatic leader seems to be almost complete, leading even to the self-sacrifice of the followers. The social-psychology of charisma can take many forms of language and activity. That is, it can be expressed in many traditions and styles of religion, from ascetic to ecstatic.

Charisma was named by Max Weber, borrowing the Greek root used prominently in Christianity to refer to special powers given to individuals by God. That is the way charisma appears to those who respond to it, namely as a transcendent, godlike authority and sacredness, with both attractive and fear-inspiring dimensions. In mild forms it would seem to be no more nor than the good feelings of trust and confidence certain people inspire. That which elicits such confidence could be such nonreligious features as physical strength, height, and erotic attractiveness, as well as features associated with trusted parents and other respected persons (friendly tone of voice, facial expression, etc.).

We begin to call the group of followers of a charismatic person a cult when the group separates itself from the surrounding community and forms total (totalitarian) alternative life structures. The charismatic leader, self-consciously or not, takes increasingly greater charge of the followers' thoughts and actions. There are many questions which are raised regarding the wisdom or morality of such a situation. One might condemn such structures whether they produce good acts and thoughts or not, because they compromise the personal integrity and autonomy of the followers. We usually become aware of these dynamics, however, when the results are not approved by the rest of the society. The most notorious example in the last few decades was Jonestown and its mass suicide.

The names for various kinds of charismatic leaders come from their particular vehicle of authority. A prophet speaks (perhaps writes) as an emissary of a god. A "spiritual director" is the director of others' lives in the cultivation of some religiously valued state or status. "Master" can be used for such a guide or it can indicate a teacher of religious life. Some words from other languages and cultures are increasingly used in English discussion for this kind of teacher-guide, e.g. *guru* (Hinduism) and *shaikh* (Islam). The shaman, seer, and diviner are other specialists recognized by religious people and put into type categories by scholars. All of these types of roles in religious groups are basically informal, spontaneous, and selective, rather than regularized or official. They are expected, recognized, and selected, but not inevitable.

When the leadership and supporting roles in groups are made a part of a formal structure, people just do not assume the role individually or by popular consent. Instead they must be elected, appointed, or otherwise publicly designated. People in these roles might have personal charisma, but the office or role itself has interpersonal authority even when the office-holder is unimpressive. Religious institutions, like any social organizations, need stability and continuity in the face of death and disability. Stability is enhanced by assigning leadership in terms of function instead of personality. Whenever a vacancy occurs, the role is filled by a new person and the function continues. Religious offices of this type include the many kinds of priests, ministers, and other professionals plus the CEOs of the various levels of operations, e.g. bishops, abbots, and presidents.

While charismatic leadership is a defining feature of a cult, official, regularized leadership has been associated with another type of religious social structure. This has been called the "church" type of religious organization. The church group is large, old, and well established. Sometimes it is actually called "established" when it is the official religion of a country. When a church type group is not formally established and competes with other church groups it is often called a "denomination." These terms come from Christian usage but can be applied to any religion, allowing for their analogous application. Thus the Buddhist *sangha* when used of the whole community of Buddhists can be churchlike.

Somewhere between the cult and the church in size and character is the type of organization which is called a "sect." To be sectioned or to have a sector illustrate the basic meaning of a sect; it is cut off from the rest. Of course, a cult is the most obviously separated and the church, the least. There is a broad range of possibilities between the two. To name a group a sect is not usually a compliment and few groups adopt the term for self-description. The fact remains, nevertheless, that many religious groups, often quite large, define themselves in part by their rejection of much in their surrounding societies and other religious groups.

All of the words reviewed so far in this chapter have been defined in the modern context of pluralism. These religious groups are universal in their scope because they can have members in any nation and are not identified necessarily with any one national group. Religious pluralism and the separation of religion from government is fairly recent in the history of humankind.

In some places today, and in many places during previous centuries and millennia, there were no specifically religious social structures because religion and culture were identical—church and state were not separate. These situations are sometimes referred to as folk religions. In this context chiefs and kings were also priests. A prominent recent example is the Japanese Shinto tradition and the role of the emperor in it. So also, fathers and mothers had religious roles. All people of the community were automatically part of the religious community, although there were different degrees and roles to be fulfilled. Roles in these natural religious communities are differentiated by gender and age. Transitions from one status to another are ritually observed. Initiation rites mark the puberty transition from child to adult. Weddings mark the transition from single to (potential) parent. Funerals are understood to be rituals of transition to the next status, that of the ancestors.

There are some religious specialists in natural religious groups. They are fairly informal and yet are recognized and expected in such societies. Examples would be the shaman, the witch-doctor, various seers or diviners. These roles are assumed by certain people voluntarily, and are given public recognition when other people relate to them in appropriate ways.

A touch of the voluntary religious organization sometimes appears in these natural religious groups. A secret society may be an optional sub-group which one joins through an initiation ritual. This can be understood as attaining a status like that of the dead while still living. The initiation into the fourth *ashrama* of Hinduism involves a legal and ritual death. Entrance into the optional monastic status in Christianity and Buddhism often involves a symbolic death.

The natural age and family identities remain religiously relevant in some voluntary religions even while attention is shifted to the specifically religious roles. In Burmese Buddhism the first stage of monastic initiation (into a liminal state) is used as a puberty rite, but monastic identities as such remain the religiously significant social roles, not the natural age status. Some voluntary religious organizations bless weddings even if married status is optional and not primarily a religious role.

Contemporary titles for offices of leadership often mirror secular structures, e.g. president, superintendent, etc. There are also names and offices peculiar to religions. The word "clergy" and its related form "cleric" are often used to name the whole category of religious professionals. Clerical workers and clerks now are associated with business offices, but the association with religious functionaries comes from past times when the clergy were the only literate people in many places.

Among the official roles and functions the term priest has been mentioned. There is an interesting etymological history here which highlights the options for religious leadership in Christianity as well as elsewhere. The English word "priest" comes from the Greek *presbyteros*, which means an elder. Thus the same word has developed into names for different kinds of leadership. A priest is a sacrificial functionary. An elder fills an administrative, teaching, or supervisory role (especially in churches often named for it, the Presbyterian tradition).

The connection between the priest and sacrifice is controversial in some Christian theologies. The issue arises in talking about the sacrifice of the Mass. In any event, a priest in any religion can be used broadly for any liturgical functionary, but it is more specifically connected with sacrifices of some sort. Thus ancient Israelite religion had priests (which translates words which do not mean elder) when it had a temple, but leaders of worship in Judaism away from Jerusalem and since the temple's destruction have not been called priests. A rabbi may be a teacher, counselor, and administrator, but does not reside over sacrifices. Buddhist monks may be drafted into various roles at lay people's ceremonies, but they too are not priests in the narrower sense of the term.

A monk or nun represents another type of religious social identity, by which we can also understand what a monastery is. Although other religions display some of these characteristics, monasticism is most prominent in Buddhism and Christianity. In the former tradition it is the core center of the group. For some Buddhist thought, only the monastics are really doing the Buddhist religion, while lay people are supporters hoping for the chance to be monastics in their future lives. The *sangha*, as noted above, can refer to the whole community of people convinced by Buddhist teaching and committed to following it in some fashion. But originally and more narrowly it names only the Buddhist monastic institution.

In Christianity, monasticism has been an alternative social structure alongside the church, offering an optional social structure to the parish and diocese, with its priests and bishops. Confusion has arisen, however, as the clergy have been monastified and the monasteries clericized. So many priests have lived a monastic lifestyle and so many monks have become priests that the distinction between them has been blurred. Monks are not necessarily priests because, as monks, they are dedicated to a kind of lifestyle. There is nothing in their rules and initiations which prescribes any ritual service for others outside their community (or themselves).

The word "monk" is derived from the Greek for being alone. Monastics have often formed communities which are highly organized social institutions. The regulations of these communities, however, have explicitly honored and promoted the solitary pursuit of holiness. In the older monastic traditions holiness has been cultivated with the chanting of sacred texts and various meditation or contemplation practices. The more recent Christian semi-monastic groups, called "religious orders," have blended such practices with other activities. Education, nursing, and missionary preaching are thus thought to be actions as important and effective as prayer in the practice of holiness.

With these brief comments on social patterns, this exploration of words used in the study of religions comes to an end. Dictionaries and encyclopedias will have to take over from here. If this book has accomplished its mission, however, you will have a context and a set of cautions for all subsequent investigations.